S0-ATH-427

Getting Elected

Getting Elected

A GUIDE TO WINNING STATE AND LOCAL OFFICE

by

Chester G. Atkins

with

Barry Hock & Bob Martin

WITHDRAWN

HOUGHTON MIFFLIN COMPANY BOSTON

1973

TYLER STATE COLLEGE LIBRARY

FIRST PRINTING   C

Copyright © 1973 by Chester G. Atkins
All rights reserved. No part of this work may
be reproduced or transmitted in any form by any means,
electronic or mechanical, including photocopying and
recording, or by any information storage or retrieval
system, without permission in writing from the publisher.

ISBN: 0-395-16614-4
Library of Congress Catalog Card Number: 72-12401
Printed in the United States of America

Foreword

To most Americans, it seems, the process of getting elected is not only foreign but also somewhat mysterious. Though the expense and energy required to organize a political campaign are in themselves important deterrents, I suspect that the overriding reason why so few citizens ever run for office is a belief that it takes an unusual person to convince his fellow citizens to vote for him. Nothing could be further from the truth, as any close observer of politics must realize.

That is the reason why this book was written: to "demystify" political campaigning and to make information about the campaign process as widely available as possible. For a candidate whose views effectively represent those of his constituency, getting elected is essentially a technical and organizational problem.

In setting out to write a book about "getting elected," I was especially anxious to show that my success in becoming the youngest legislator in Massachusetts history was not due to any unusual set of circumstances or to any special talent on my part. It was simply the result of doing methodically and well what candidates throughout the nation do every year. The fundamental message of this book, if there is one, is that political office is within the reach of almost any citizen who takes the time and trouble to run.

My own political education occurred in the time-honored

manner: After taking part in the Vietnam Summer movement of 1967, I worked as a storefront manager in the McCarthy campaign of 1968 in Indiana, Wisconsin and Oregon. Later that year I managed the Congressional campaign of Robert Cecile in Springfield, Ohio. In 1970 I sought and won a state representative seat in Massachusetts, and in 1972 I was elected to the state senate.

What I have learned about the art of campaigning in the past several years is not unique. Candidates have known for generations that knocking on doors and handing out leaflets are the nuts and bolts of politics. The material contained in this book does not represent a radically new perspective on campaigning; it is simply a systematic presentation of information that any good political worker should know.

In conclusion, I should like to make grateful acknowledgment to at least a few of the many individuals whose advice and assistance made this book possible: Massachusetts State Representative John Businger, who gave generously of his time in discussing various campaign problems; John Gorman of Cambridge Survey Research, who provided helpful advice on political polling; and Alison Lauriat, my administrative assistant, who contributed greatly to several sections of the book.

CHESTER G. ATKINS

Contents

Introduction

THIS BOOK is addressed to the countless liberals and activists whose idealism and dedication during the last ten years have aroused the moral conscience of America and begun to make "participatory democracy" a byword of the nation's politics.

It was written with two basic premises: that local and state politics and government deserve far more attention than they have been given by most of the people taking part in the issue-oriented movements of the past decade; and that what has come to be collectively known among young people as "The Movement" will have permanent importance in American politics only if those who created it take the vital step of running for office themselves instead of merely trying to influence those already in office.

The Emphasis on National Politics

The mass movements of the sixties tapped and united a vast constituency for social change in America. That change will come about, however, only if those who seek it begin to accumulate political power wherever it is available. And political power is most readily available on the local or state level, where it can be had almost for the asking, not on the national level, where it must be long and carefully nurtured. Only a handful of citizens can ever hope to serve in national office, but local and state offices are readily attainable to those who are willing to do the hard work of political organization.

Paradoxically, most of the idealistic young who have become involved in politics in recent years have sought national political power instead of local power, which would have been far easier to obtain. They have tended to ignore or bypass local politics and attempted to bring about social change mainly by bringing pressure on national government. Rather than focus attention on city hall, the county courthouse, or the state capitol, young activists have a tendency to perceive every problem as a national problem, and have for the most part sought national solutions.

Congressmen and Presidents in the past ten years have been continuously besieged with demands for immediate action on problems ranging from the Vietnam war to still important but basically local problems such as rat control. Local officials, by contrast, have generally been left to go about business as usual, facing serious challenge by New Left or New Politics factions only in short-lived crises. Though members of civil rights, anti-war, and other organizations have often been deeply committed to working in congressional or presidential campaigns, few of them have become involved in local campaigns or politics.

There are a number of explanations for this tendency to look to Washington for solutions to all social problems. Probably the most important element in starting this trend was the fact that the early civil rights and anti-war groups, which spawned a host of other organizations, did have to look to Washington.

Reinforcing this tendency to look to national government was the sense of strength and solidarity that resulted from being able to put 100,000 people into Washington for a demonstration. Small groups in campuses and communities across the land believed they were more influential as members of a nationwide movement of millions rather than as isolated local caucuses of only fifty or a hundred people.

Another ingredient in the trend was the simple fact that information about national government is more readily accessible than in the case of local government: television, newspapers, and books provide far better data on national government than on local government, making it easier for most people to know what goes on in the White House than to know what their city council is doing.

The recent emphasis on the power of Federal government to solve any problem also reflects the frequent financial dependency of local and state government on national government. In 1969, 57.3 per cent of all governmental expenditures on all levels were made by the Federal government. Hardly a governmental program exists on any level today without some form of Federal financial aid. Local schools, highways, hospitals, and other facilities are seldom built without Federal support. Where Federal money is not a factor, Federal law often is, since many local programs — such as legal aid to the poor — are inspired by either national legislation or Supreme Court decisions. It is hardly surprising that the various movements — in ecology, education, and prison reform — should follow the lead of mayors and governors in seeking national solutions to problems that rightly should have been dealt with on the local level.

By the end of the sixties, however, it had become clear that a) the emphasis on national government was in many cases misdirected and b) in those areas where Federal action had been taken, it was necessary to see that national policy was being implemented on the local and state levels. Working solely on the Federal level, it was apparent, would not solve problems created by officials on the local level. For example, passage of the Voting Rights Act of 1964 did not guarantee that local registrars would seek out new voters. Political activists throughout the country have therefore begun to devote increased attention to local and state government.

Local Limits on National Power

In attaching so much importance to national politics, both liberal and radical theorists have tended to overlook other realities about political power in the United States. Compared to the power of local government, the power of the Federal government is much more limited than it might seem at first glance.

There are only 537 elected Federal officials but there are more than half a million local elective offices in the United States. In 1970, there were 508,720 locally elected officials and 13,038 elected state officials (most of whom are legislators elected in local races).

Local Elective Offices in the United States, 1970

County	74,199
Municipal	143,927
Township	129,603
School	107,663
Special Districts (utility, recreation & other)	56,943
State	13,038

Similarly, the number of Federal civilian employees is small in comparison to the number of workers employed by local and state governments. Of 12.8 million civilian government employees in the United States in 1970, only 2.7 million were employed by the Federal government, less than one fourth of the total. Another 2.7 million were employed by state government, while 7.4 million were employed by other local government agencies.

For all the emphasis on the Federal government's power of

the purse, local and state governments do have the power to raise and spend money for most of the purposes for which they seek Federal funds. Many state governments fail to use the income tax or make little use of other types of taxes, but they have most of the powers of taxation that the Federal government has. In many cases they simply decline to use that power.

All but 10,522 of the 81,248 local governmental units in existence in 1967 had the power to raise funds by means of the property tax, not to mention other means of taxation. The local and state officials who cry loudest for Federal aid are often merely seeking to avoid the political problem of increasing local taxes. If the Federal government has financial power over state and local agencies, it is primarily because state and local politicians have all too gladly abdicated both their power and the responsibility that goes with it.

The financial power of the Federal government, moreover, is vastly overrated in most discussions of local and state programs. Federal funds may account for more than half of governmental expenditures in the country, but most of what the Federal government spends goes into military and foreign affairs or into programs such as Social Security or government pensions. Local and state expenditures account for most of the money spent on basic public services such as education, sewerage systems, police and fire protection.

Federal aid to education, for example, has received far more publicity and far more credit than it deserves. Of the 43 billion dollars spent on public elementary and secondary education in the United States in 1971, only three billion consisted of Federal funds. State governments provided another 16 billion dollars, while the largest share, 24 billion, was raised and spent by local government.

Out of sheer gratitude to Congress for funding their pet projects, educators have created the impression that Federal aid to education is far more substantial and significant than it really is. In most communities, Federally financed educational services are merely the frosting on the cake of locally financed services. Lost in the shuffle in various debates about the need for Federal aid is the fact that local officials have the power to initiate any educational program they wish. Municipal and county school boards call all the shots in educational policy-making in most places and Federal aid is needed only to the extent that local officials are afraid to increase local taxes.

In terms of both money and educational policy, educational reformers are barking up the wrong tree when they look to Washington for basic changes in the nation's schools. The Federal government does fund a few desirable programs that would otherwise not exist, but it does not control most of what is done in education.

In other areas such as urban planning, pollution control, or racial integration, local officials are responsible for financing and executing most of the programs which concern nationally oriented reformers. Local officials have the power to carry most of the burdens the national government is implored to take up, but they are unwilling to take responsibility for such programs. There are national dimensions to any of the public problems that face local communities, but solutions to these problems must be implemented on the local level.

Federal leadership, moreover, is no substitute for local initiative. The President and the Congress can do what they will to urge the nation forward in causes such as building decent housing, but it is up to the millions of local government officials throughout the nation to see that federally initiated programs are properly implemented. No amount of national legislation eliminates the need for cooperation with Federal laws on the part of local officials. The attitudes of many police officials toward Supreme Court decisions such as *Miranda* ought to be ample testimony to this point.

The success of any Federal program depends above all on the reception it gets from local officials. The Federal food stamp program is a case in point. Officials in many towns and counties throughout the nation have often simply declined to handle food stamps, thus depriving poor people of a major income supplement. In other programs, such as Federal housing loans or unemployment benefits, local agencies often play the crucial role of deciding who gets benefits and to what extent. Even the best Federal leadership can be thwarted by hostile local officials.

Much can be done in Washington to change the course of the nation for good or ill, but the cooperation of local officials is almost invariably essential to the success of Federal undertakings. The power of Washington is quite real, but its extent is an illusion encouraged by those seeking quick solutions or by local officials anxious to pass the buck.

The fact that the political fortunes of national leaders are based on intricate pyramids of local political power is too often overlooked. In campaigns such as that of Eugene McCarthy against Lyndon Johnson, liberal activists have often ignored the existence of these pyramids and merely sought to lop off the peaks in the hope that the whole structure would then collapse. Though McCarthy helped force Johnson out of office, he lacked the local contacts and loyalties that provide every national leader with a political base. It thus does a national leader little good to be full of fresh ideas if the foundation on which his power rests is hostile to those ideas. National leaders, also, usually are recruited from the ranks of local political organizations and rise only because of the support they have gathered on the local level.

The Power of Local Officials

There is a lot more power and opportunity to accomplish something in local politics than nationally oriented activists have generally recognized. The most important limits to what a local political organization can achieve have to do with its size and effectiveness, not with the cooperation of state and Federal officials. Liberal activists need to give much more thought to the possibilities of local action than they generally have.

From secrecy in government to health care or transportation, any issue (other than foreign policy issues) important on the national level is likely to be important on the local level as well. Most police departments throughout the country, for example, are involved in surveillance of citizens thought by state or national officials to be radical or "subversive." School boards, city councils, and other such agencies do much of their business in secret, while any city with major industry contains the seeds of corruption which the ITT affair of 1972 typified on the national level.

It does not require Federal legislation for a local agency to institute pioneering programs in pollution control, transportation, health care, or integration. The plight of migrant workers on farms throughout the nation is a good example of a problem in which national solutions are widely demanded while local action could be taken more quickly. The wretched shacks in which migrant workers usually live could not exist if municipal building codes were written so as to eliminate squalid conditions and then were enforced. The cycle of ignorance and poverty which causes migrant children to grow into migrant laborers could be broken if school officials provided educational services and other local agencies provided the rest of the services available to most citizens.

The same is true with numerous other national problems. City and town sewage systems, for example, are among the major polluters of the nation's rivers and streams. Local planning boards often play the decisive role in determining whether a town remains an attractive and congenial place for people to live or is allowed to be overrun by industrialists, strip-miners, housing developers, or others seeking a quick profit at the cost of destroying a community. The corruption of a building inspector can be enough to create a slum, while the difference between a pond which becomes a major recreational center and one which becomes a cesspool, can be the simple difference between a good local conservation commission and a poor one.

The list of possibilities for constructive local programs is as long as the list of the nation's problems. Anyone with his eyes riveted on what the leadership in Washington is planning to do about such problems should also investigate the potential for action in his own community.

Local Office Is Available

Ultimately, the most important point in this discussion of Federal vs. local political power is that municipal, county, or state office is often available to just about anyone who wants it. Liberal youth in particular in the past decade have spent their political talent and energy mainly on trying to elect *other people* into *national* office, rather than seeking local office *themselves*. This pattern has existed both because the more liberal activists have not felt it possible to elect anyone from among their own numbers into national office, and because they have not regarded local office as worth seeking. In both cases the result has been that the young liberals who have done the basic work of campaigning have not put anyone into office who actually represents their views. In ignoring local politics, young people have for the most part passed up their best opportunity to gain actual political power.

As the rest of this book will make clear, running for office is never simple or easy. A local campaign can be as demanding on a candidate and his supporters as any larger campaign.

But since most local campaigns involve much smaller electorates than a congressional campaign, it is less costly to run for local office and a local campaign can be waged by a far smaller staff. As a result, local politics is a game that anyone can play. A novice can be a candidate on the local level, whereas in a congressional, statewide or national campaign, he or she would be relegated to working in some minor and politically insignificant capacity.

The material presented in this book was prepared solely with local elections in mind, especially those in which the electoral district involves not more than about 100,000 residents. It thus should be useful for candidates for municipal or county office in almost every section of the country, as well as state legislature candidates in most areas. The emphasis throughout the following chapters is on running a campaign on the lowest possible budget, but with maximum use of volunteer labor.

The campaign techniques discussed here are those which have been described by the media as the style of "The New Politics." There is little that is new about these techniques, however. Precinct by precinct and block by block canvassing are as old as American politics. While some of the trappings of campaigning may have changed, candidates on the stump operate no differently today than they did 150 years ago. Perhaps the main distinction that can be made between the old and the "new" politics lies in who takes part. The past few years have seen a major influx of candidates who had previously been shut out of the political system. Some of those had been shut out for reasons of age, race or sex; others by their lack of money or lack of connections with the small groups of men who treated electoral offices as club posts which only the initiate could be permitted to enter. One by one, the barriers to mass participation in politics have begun to fall.

Even where the barriers to participatory politics have been

lowered, however, one final hurdle usually remains: the ignorance or inexperience of citizens who feel shut out of politics
by their own bewilderment at the way the electoral system
works. The purpose of this book, then, is to make information
about the techniques involved in running a campaign available to any citizen who has an interest in running for office but
has not given expression to that interest for lack of information.

Getting Elected

/ 7

1

The Decision to Run

BECOMING A CANDIDATE for office is one of the most ambitious steps any citizen interested in public affairs can take. It is also potentially one of the most rewarding. Because of the extremely demanding nature of both campaigning and serving in office, however, becoming a candidate is a step that no one should take lightly.

Running for office can require months of concentrated effort. Victory is only one of two possibilities awaiting a candidate: there is no compromise between victory and defeat. And even when victory is attained, the morning after election day is merely the beginning of a candidate's real task: to prove he meant what he said in his months of campaigning.

The first question any prospective candidate must ask himself, therefore, is what kind of commitment he is willing to make to the long-term process of getting elected and then serving in office. On any level, running for office requires a much greater commitment of time and energy than most of the public ever realizes.

No one gets elected to office without putting in long hours at such frustrating chores as shaking hands, attending dinners or rallies, and rounding up material or financial support. No one elected to office can hope to accomplish much without dedicating further long hours to attending meetings, making endless numbers of phone calls, and constantly striving to be ready for the next crisis or the next opportunity.

A candidate needs to base his decision to run for office on quite real questions such as what kind of work week the job requires, whether he is temperamentally suited to the pace and nature of the work, and what impact his political involvement will have on his personal life, his job, and his general well-being. If the office he is seeking is a part-time job, can he afford to devote three or four nights a week to attending and following up on weekly meetings? If the job is full time, will he be able to live on the officeholder's salary? Will performing the job mean neglecting a family? The commitment demanded of a candidate is not a matter of abstract moral principles alone, but a question of whether entering politics is compatible with leading what he considers a good life.

Reasons for Running

There are probably as many reasons for running for office as there are candidates, including such commonplace reasons as enjoying being in the public eye or relishing the intensity of political life. Leaving such factors aside, however, the reasons for running for office can be summed up in terms of three basic types of candidacy: the single-issue candidate; the symbolic candidate; and the candidate who plans to be permanently or at least indefinitely involved in politics.

A. The Single-Issue Candidate

Many a candidate is drawn into politics as a result of his interest in a single issue or narrow range of issues about which he either feels very strongly or thinks he knows more than the other candidates. A good example is the citizen whose concern for his children's education leads him to run for a school board seat after the firing of a liberal school superintendent by a conservative board. Though not particularly knowledgeable about the details of various educational problems, the candidate decides to run in order to seek reinstatement of the superintendent and to prevent the board from drastically changing the school system.

Two points about this candidate are immediately clear: first, that his choice of which office to seek is unalterable — there is no other office in which he could accomplish his objective; second, it is quite possible that running for office is not necessarily the most effective way for him to achieve his goal (even if elected, he may still face a conservative majority on the board).

Whether this type of candidate is wise to run for office depends very much on local circumstances, particularly on what other options are available. It could well be easier and simpler to work through an existing organization such as the PTA, or even to start a new organization of concerned citizens with the express goal of reinstating the superintendent.

Another factor such a candidate should consider is that anyone who is truly a single-issue candidate is unlikely to get elected unless he is voicing a particularly strong community sentiment not articulated by other candidates. The anti-busing candidate is a prime example of a one-issue candidate who could well get elected without even discussing other issues. When less emotional issues dominate a campaign, however, a candidate's lack of interest or knowledge regarding matters other than his own obsession will be obvious to the voters and will be a liability for his candidacy. Equally important, a person who is really interested in only one issue is not going to make much of an officeholder, and may be doing the public a disservice by seeking election.

A second type of single-issue candidate also deserves mention here: namely, the candidate whose issue is not relevant to the office he is seeking. An anti-war spokesman running for a seat in the state legislature with the war as his main issue may appeal to a large number of voters but still fail to get their votes. If he doesn't see that there is very little a state legislator could do about the war, the voters certainly will. Similarly, a candidate whose greatest concern is the unfairness of the local property tax should not be running for a school board seat.

Of course, a candidate for the legislature might very well point out that the war has resulted in the scarcity of Federal funds for state programs. Or a school board candidate might note that the use of the property tax to finance schools is the reason why there are major differences in the quality of schools from one community to another. Nevertheless, neither of these candidates would be able to remedy the problem he is concerned with through the office he is seeking. Such a candidate is condemning himself to frustration — if not to defeat — by concerning himself with the wrong office at the outset.

A final point concerning single-issue candidates is that any candidate who identifies himself with only one issue is putting himself in a box. The single-issue candidate is likely to be as ephemeral as his issue.

B. The Symbolic Candidate

In contrast to the single-issue candidate who runs in the hope of winning an election, another type of candidate popular in American politics is the candidate who runs not to win but to achieve some long range purpose such as educating the public on an issue or mobilizing a particular constituency. This type of candidate also jeopardizes his political future by risking that he will not be taken seriously.

It has long been the tradition of issue-oriented movements to run or endorse candidates representing their views. This phenomenon recurs so often because the "campaign" orientation and strategy has many advantages as a form of political organizing. The public understands candidacies and campaigns much more readily than it does diffuse, issue-oriented organizing. As a symbol of the issue, a candidate may be easier for the public to understand than the issue itself. A candidacy is also tangible and measurable: it has a goal (winning the election), a deadline (election day), and a defined constituency (the district). It is simpler for voters to respond to a symbolic candidacy than to follow an issue through months or years of political maneuver.

Symbolic candidacies certainly can be successful. Eugene McCarthy's 1968 campaign produced significant changes in the Democratic Party's war policy, and in the process it assembled a nationwide machine of young and liberal campaigners whose subsequent availability formed the basis of numerous local and national candidacies since then.

On the local level, a symbolic candidacy might be used to weld together the members of a minority group not previously counted as politically important in its community. For example, a student running in a mayoralty primary in a community with a sizeable student population might be able to land enough votes to force other candidates to deal with an issue such as rent control. There are numerous variations on this type of candidacy, which is by no means new to American politics.

As effective as the symbolic candidacy can be, conditions for its success are not always present. An electorate which is generally satisfied with the performance of its politicians is not likely to respond very well to a candidate concerned less with winning than with mounting a protest. No voter likes to know that he is throwing away his vote, even though he may be willing to vote for a dark-horse candidate. A voter is not likely to take the trouble to get to the polls unless there seems to be something to vote for that reflects his sentiments.

A political campaign normally exists for the sole purpose of winning enough votes to put a candidate into office, and it is important that campaign workers believe they are taking part in an effort that will win. A campaign working for any other goal is settling for one degree or another of defeat. It makes little sense to stage a symbolic campaign unless the symbol is one that may have wide appeal and will be understood by both the voters and the other candidates.

C. Permanent Involvement

Most candidates are not obsessed with a particular issue, not irrevocably committed to seeking a particular office, and not interested in anything less than winning an election. Most of those entering politics do not do so with the intention of giving it up after serving one or two terms in office: most candidates look upon politics as a permanent or at least indefinite commitment, if not in fact as a career.

The candidate with a permanent interest in politics has much more latitude in choosing an office and in deciding when to run than do symbolic or single-issue candidates. He also needs to make wiser choices than they do, since he is more concerned about "staying alive" as a political leader. He cannot afford to be reckless or quixotic in his decisions as to when and where to run.

Choosing an Office

Any prospective candidate whose mind is not absolutely set on what office to seek should take a close look at the full range of offices available in his community. There are always a wide variety of local offices, and many of them are posts that are all but forgotten by most citizens between elections. Positions such as town clerk, auditor, or tax assessor may have little visibility during the political off-season, but they are important posts in many communities, and seldom without power. The job of a tax assessor might sound dull and routine, but it can be an excellent post in which to learn the impact of municipal financial policy on various groups and then to develop a program of tax reform. Before making his decision, any candidate should consider all the options available. A candidate who takes a creative approach to a routine job can quickly make a name for himself.

This is not to say that any candidate should run for an office which does not interest him. No one should run just for the sake of running, since a candidate's lack of interest or dedication will both decrease his own enthusiasm and eventually become apparent to the public. Likewise, no one should run for an office only because it seems to be a decent steppingstone to another post. Such a candidate may gain a reputation as an opportunist, and probably will not be happy even if he gets elected.

On the other hand, the variety of offices available in any community provides anyone interested in public affairs a number of options at each election season. If one office is unavailable for some reason, there is likely to be some other office in which the candidate will see an opportunity to accomplish something.

Once again, it is necessary to stress that a candidate should run for the office which interests him most, unless there is a decisive reason not to, such as when the incumbent is of the same party, is doing a good job, or differs little from the prospective candidate. Waiting is often a costly error in politics, since political conditions can turn about very quickly. Any candidate who passes up an obvious opportunity may discover when the next election comes around that the office has become locked up by someone else, or that an opponent who was previously nowhere to be seen has suddenly become formidable.

Can the Seat Be Won?

Whether a seat can be won is a crucial question for any candidate. While no newcomer to politics can safely guess what his own vote-getting ability will be, there are a number of related types of information he can readily obtain. How similar candidates have faired in the past, what firm support the opponent has, and what support is up for grabs are questions it is relatively simple to answer.

One of the first places a candidate should look to determine his chances of being elected is in past election records. Analysis of voting patterns will be discussed at length in the next chapter. While the estimate of voting strength that a candidate makes in May might not even closely resemble the final results, it should be sufficient to tell him whether it is worthwhile to enter the race.

A second source of information about a candidate's prospects for election is community leadership — in both social and political organizations. Leaders of community groups of any kind have contact with a wide enough sampling of voters and other leaders to help a candidate evaluate his standing in the community. Since the same sources are also valuable as potential supporters, their reactions are also significant as indicators of his viability. The president of a Kiwanis Club, taxpayers' association, or similar organization may not be a political seer, but he is likely to understand the local power structure and to have a feel for public opinion. Such leaders therefore make good sounding boards for anyone considering candidacy. (This is not to say that a candidate who meets the general opposition of established community leaders should give up the idea of running. But where that is the case, a candidate should have a clear idea of where his support *will* come from before he decides to run.)

Another way for a candidate to judge his own prospects is to find out who his opponent's enemies are. Since no one in public life can please everyone, any well-known politician is certain to have alienated some segments of his community. Any candidate can include the enemies of his opponent among his own potential supporters. (This principle has its limits, however: while it might be convenient for a liberal candidate to learn that the Sierra Club is infuriated by a mayor's lack of interest in conservation, it would not be of much value to a liberal to find that the local John Birch Society considers his opponent a fellow traveler.)

Promises of support or other encouragement from the people he consults are important indicators of a candidate's potential strength. Words of encouragement, however, should be regarded as cautiously as advice until they begin to be translated into material support. Just as no candidate should let himself be dissuaded from running solely by a poor reception from entrenched community leadership, he should also avoid letting their approval inflate his opinion of himself.

Apart from the expressed encouragement or opposition he may encounter among community leaders, a candidate should also take a realistic look at what his election would *mean* for them. Where the changes that his election would bring coincide with the interests of an individual or group, he can expect some degree of support, and should pursue it. Where his election would jeopardize any group's interest, he can of course expect opposition.

Other Considerations

In addition to finding out whether the office he has his eye on can be won, a prospective candidate should be sure to learn whether it is already spoken for by someone whose claim he ought to respect. In one sense, this means only that a candidate should be certain to identify all others who may be running for the same office and to find out how powerful their support is. But it also means that he should avoid opposing a candidate with whom he basically agrees and who has the support of elements whose interest must be recognized.

The first such situation is the conventional problem of "bucking the party," a dilemma that anyone new to a community's political scene is likely to face. What constitutes bucking the party differs greatly from one area to another. In an all-Democratic community, for example, the only election worthy of the name may be the Democratic primary. In that case it may not be considered bad form to oppose the party's nominee, even if he is an incumbent.

The only way of resolving the dilemma of bucking the party is to have a talk with party officials or with the other candidates seeking the nomination. It may be that some mutually agreeable way of coming to a decision and avoiding a primary fight can be arranged. Even if that is not the case, a candidate will still have come to a better understanding of his situation and of the opposition he faces.

No candidate should challenge an incumbent of his own party unless there are serious differences of opinion between the two or there are other good reasons for doing so. A candidate who does challenge a member of his own party for no apparent reason other than personal ambition may be seen as an opportunist, split the party, and hand the election to the opposing party. That development would benefit no one.

Pretty much the same principles apply to community forces other than political parties. Much of the time the decision whether to oppose a like-minded candidate boils down to an ethical dilemma having little to do with the likelihood of victory per se. Take for example the problem facing a white liberal thinking of running in an election where a black community leader is running for the first time. On one hand, it may be that if both run they will split the liberal vote in such a way as to hand a conservative the election. On the other hand, even if the white liberal is able to win, he is guaranteeing that it will be at least a few more years before the black community has any elected leadership. The decision to run in such a situation is as much a moral decision as a question of practical politics.

None of the above is intended as a flat prohibition against bucking the system, nor as a statement that a candidate should retreat at the first sign of an opponent who appears to be an equally good candidate. It is merely a warning that no candidate should wander blithely into a race where he does not know who and what he is opposing. It might turn out that the forces he is opposing would like to have him on their side, or that they are the very sources of support he will most need on his side in the long run.

The only way to discover such problems is to become acquainted with members of various political groups and thus tune in on the political grapevine. A candidate who speaks to his expected opponent before making his plans public may very well find out that the opponent is in fact about to retire or seek another office. Instead of finding hostility, he may pick up some unexpected assistance. The worst that could result from such a meeting would be an agreement to disagree.

Party Affiliation

Discussion of party affiliation or party endorsement may have little meaning to people coming into conventional politics from movement-oriented political backgrounds. A great many young activists have come to scorn the national parties, often for quite justifiable reasons. But parties have been in disrepute since George Washington warned the nation to dismantle them — obviously to no avail. The fact remains that in most cases it is necessary to belong to a political party in order to be regarded as a serious candidate.

The sole valid reason for running as an independent is that it is the only way to get elected to a particular office — that is, if there is literally no opportunity of getting elected otherwise.

A candidate who gets elected as an independent will have to come to terms with political parties anyway, and being an independent will simply mean that he has no natural allies. The political compromises an independent is likely to have to make are just as numerous as those he would have to make in joining a party. The problems he is likely to face will limit his achievements more than enough to outweigh his reasons for not joining a party. And once an individual has operated as an independent he is likely to have great difficulty if he ever decides to join a party.

Deciding which party to choose can be a dilemma, since the choice is permanent. Unlike a voter, a candidate is not free to switch parties at will in the secrecy of a voting booth. It is not very often that a politician can reverse his choice of parties without serious consequences for his future.

What usually makes party choice especially difficult is the fact that party programs and ideology are so often different on the local level from what they are on the national level. A liberal candidate in a community dominated by conservative Democrats may very well regard the local Republican faction with favor — especially if it seems that the Republican nomination could be had for the asking while it would take a bitter primary fight to make victory as a Democrat possible.

In such a situation any candidate is in a dilemma that he can only resolve for himself. A candidate with modest ambitions might do best to follow the path of least resistance in choosing his party — basing his decision solely on local party positions. A candidate with any thought of higher office is wise to base his decision on his sympathy for the national parties.

Before leaving the subject of parties it is necessary to note that in many states local elections are contested on a nonpartisan basis. That is, candidates for local office are not permitted to use party affiliation in their campaigns.

Even where this practice is mandated by law, however, parties often play a key role in elections. Candidates may be discretely chosen and endorsed by party organizations and may work closely with party officials in campaigning and carrying out their duties after being elected. It is thus necessary to be just as watchful for party influence in "nonpartisan" elections as in openly partisan contests.

Credibility

Of all the factors entering into a first-time candidate's decision to run, his credibility as a candidate should probably be the most important. Credibility is the measure of how seriously a candidate is taken by opponents, by potential supporters, and ultimately by the voters.

Several ingredients go into the making of a credible candidate: experience, knowledge, exposure, and support. What a candidate may lack in one he can make up in another, but each is essential in some degree in order to make a successful appeal to the electorate. Of the four ingredients, experience is the key factor, since it usually forms the basis of each of the others.

Experience in electoral politics is not essential for a candidate, but it certainly will help. Many people involved in politics prefer to support a candidate who has "toiled in the vineyards" — which is a sign that the candidate is both committed and aware of what he is getting himself into. Taking part in another political campaign as a worker is a valuable preparation for being a candidate, since it is a convenient means of getting experience and becoming known to politically involved members of a community. It is also a means of identifying and obtaining support for one's own candidacy.

Experience in working with volunteer groups similar to a campaign organization is also a valuable asset for a candidate or his staff. Unless he has an experienced campaign manager, a complete novice may have too much to learn about managing people to be able to succeed in running a campaign the first time.

Experience in community organizations of some kind is also a virtual necessity in order to be a *credible* candidate. Working in community groups is an invaluable means of learning local problems and coming to understand the community power structure, as well as of meeting potential supporters. Any prospective candidate would therefore do well to become active in organizations such as the Jaycees or the League of Women Voters or in a specialized action group such as an organization lobbying for low-income housing.

Exposure, support, and knowledge are all exceptionally difficult to acquire for a candidate who has had little or no contact with community organizations in the past. While there is no reason why any well-informed and capable citizen could not perform well in office, his chances of getting elected are slim if he is not trusted or known by at least a few of a community's usual leaders.

It is impossible to generalize about how much support a candidate should have before deciding to embark on a campaign. Those whose support is most important are often unwilling to commit themselves until they see how well a campaign is going. A candidate should at least be able to feel that he will not get a reception that amounts to "Who are you?" from people whose support he needs. To avoid that embarrassment and to avoid seeming presumptuous, any would-be candidate should establish some reputation in his community before trying to get elected.

Money

Money is the center of a vicious circle in campaigning, since it takes money to get a campaign going and it takes a promising campaign to attract money. While it is seldom possible for any honest candidate to say at the beginning of a campaign where he will find the money he needs, it is possible to make a good estimate of what is needed.

Probably the best general policy is to figure out how much money is needed to bring the campaign to the point where it has a momentum of its own. When the seed money is obtained, a campaign can begin on the assumption that if there is any chance of winning it will be possible to come up with the balance needed to run the campaign.

It is impossible to overstress the need for caution on the part of a candidate whose personal financial situation is shaky before the campaign begins. Many a candidate commits himself to a campaign, starts to smell victory, and then spends far more of his own money on the campaign than he can actually afford. For a candidate with family responsibilities or other financial problems, that course of action could be disastrous — even if he won.

A Final Assessment

As pointed out in the beginning of this chapter, no one should leap into a political campaign with the impression that getting elected is easy. Being a candidate involves a lot of hard work and personal sacrifice, much more than most politicians ever get credit for. In addition to the strain that political life is likely to put on himself and his family, a candidate should also think of the sacrifices of those who will work for him. He must also look well beyond the election to be sure that the goal he is seeking in the campaign is really worth the effort.

No matter how committed a candidate may be to his goals he owes it to himself and his supporters to make a completely hard-nosed assessment of whether it is possible to win. That means he must take as objective a look as possible at his overall assets and liabilities.

In addition to the numerous factors mentioned in this chapter, he must also consider such subjective and personal factors as whether his name and ethnic background make getting elected improbable. There are places in America where it might be impossible for a Jew or Chinese citizen to get elected, not to mention blacks, Puerto Ricans, or Chicanos. In some communities it is impossible for a person not born in town to get elected, while in others a new arrival is not in the least handicapped. Even such factors as whether his children attend school in town, whether he is married, or where he works can be important to a candidate's prospects. A well-staged campaign can compensate for any of these factors, but a candidate must at least recognize at the outset whether they exist.

In short, a prospective candidate must not only count up his resources but must look critically at every possible obstacle to his election. Once the campaign begins, any candidate is likely to deceive himself about his chances of getting elected, and so are his supporters. The time for objectivity is before a decision is made to run.

2

Precampaign Activities

THE TIMING of a candidate's announcement involves a lot more than beating other potential candidates to the punch. Contrary to the impression created by presidential candidates, who sometimes seem to launch campaigns with no more effort than it takes to set up a speaking tour, there is a great deal of work a candidate must do before making his announcement. This does not mean that any candidate will be able to keep his intention to run a secret. The smaller his community, the more likely it is that his plans will be known well before he makes a formal announcement. Even when the news is out, there are often good reasons for delaying an announcement.

The difference between a declared candidate and an undeclared candidate is that the former is treated like a candidate and is expected to act like a candidate, while the latter can escape the pressure of public expectations. Any candidate should be actively running from the moment that he formally declares his candidacy, and that means that he must be prepared to run before making an announcement.

A candidate who makes his announcement before he has done the work necessary to be a credible candidate and to begin campaigning runs the risk of being dismissed out of hand, both by the public and by potential supporters. Having started off on the wrong foot, he will be hard pressed to overcome that bad impression.

In addition to the work any candidate ought to do before making an announcement, there is a great deal of precampaign work that can be done far more easily by a noncandidate than by a candidate. A good example is newspaper coverage. Once an editor knows that someone is a candidate, he is likely to be more sparing with news space about him and more critical in whatever coverage is given. A "concerned citizen" speaking on a public issue may be considered somewhat of a novelty and be given generous coverage. A candidate for office is not much of a curiosity to an editor, and may find it difficult to get deep or frequent coverage, especially in the early stages of a campaign. This is particularly true of TV and radio coverage, due to the "equal time" provisions of the FCC.

It is also much easier for a noncandidate to get certain kinds of information than for a candidate. A public employee may be reluctant to talk freely to someone about to run against his boss, for example. There are also people who might avoid contact with a candidate in order to avoid giving the impression that he has their endorsements, such as leaders of nonpartisan community organizations.

There are a variety of tasks for any candidate to work on before making an announcement. The nature of such tasks is the subject of this chapter.

Learning the Job

The first task for any would-be candidate is to learn as much as possible about the job he is seeking and the issues surrounding it. In addition to the obvious aspects of any political office, there are bound to be legal and administrative powers and limitations of which a candidate is unaware. There are also likely to be powers that go completely unused because of the incumbent's ignorance or indifference. The only way to learn about such matters is by doing a lot of painstaking research, starting with a check on the statutory or constitutional description of the powers of office.

A. Public Boards

A candidate seeking a seat on a committee that meets publicly is in a better position to do precampaign research than candidates for other types of office. Any such candidate should attend public meetings of the board from the moment he decides to run. Doing so provides a good picture of the personal requirements of the job — in terms of time, talent and energy — and is a good means of building a fund of campaign issues.

In addition to taking notes and obtaining copies of the minutes of such meetings, the candidate should also obtain copies of press releases, subcommittee reports and other documents prepared or used by the board. Performance and contracting records, planning studies, and other such publications can be vitally important to understanding the job and documenting arguments on campaign issues. It is also wise to keep accurate records of board attendance and votes.

In addition to information available from observing the board itself, further data can be obtained from private or public agencies with which the board does business. Most official boards hold membership in county, regional, or state associations which in turn may print a variety of periodicals and reports.

A local planning board, for example, is likely to work in conjunction with other boards in nearby communities, as well as to be linked to a regional, state, or Federal planning agency. Knowing the activities of such groups may yield a wealth of new ideas which the local board has not implemented or explored.

In conducting this research, a candidate insures that he

knows both existing policy and a wide range of possible approaches to issues, including ideas even an incumbent might be unaware of. He makes it possible to begin on an equal footing with other board members as soon as he steps into office, instead of having to go through an apprenticeship.

Another advantage in attending such meetings is the opportunity to get acquainted with other public officials and interested citizens. The candidate has a chance to make contacts that may prove useful at a later date.

B. Executive Office

Studying the performance and the duties of an administrator such as a sheriff or a mayor — or any job where the bulk of the work is done behind closed doors — is more difficult than in the case of a board that meets publicly. It may be necessary to rely more heavily on newspaper accounts and even hearsay to gain information.

With proper effort it is possible to obtain a reasonably detailed profile of any officeholder's performance and then to identify areas where he has been either effective or negligent. Once again it is good procedure to start with copies of public documents such as budget reports, program plans and studies and press releases. Professional associations are frequently good sources of new ideas.

To learn about any local problem, it is often possible to get data from state agencies. If a mayor has done nothing about a housing shortage, for example, it might be a good idea to consult state or Federal housing agencies to see what opportunities the mayor has neglected.

A study of a department's budget records will often yield a good understanding of what the department's priorities and problems are, or at least point to areas that need to be investigated further. While such a study may not reveal outright corruption or mismanagement, it may reveal who the incumbent's supporters are. The identities of his appointees and of the suppliers or contractors doing business with his department may provide clues as to who the incumbent's friends are.

By knowing a great deal about the details of a department's operation a candidate can develop serious proposals for more efficient administration, better service, or new programs.

C. *Legislative Office*

Learning what a legislator has been doing can be more difficult than finding out what goes on at city hall or the county courthouse, particularly if the state capital is several hundred miles away. On the other hand, it is easier to point up a legislator's failings, since he does not have a department beneath him in which to hide his shortcomings.

The starting point for studying a legislator's performance is to obtain copies of all the bills he has filed from the State House. A list of the incumbent's bills should be available from either his own office or from public documents. It should also be possible to obtain an incumbent's voting record.

Once copies of the incumbent's bills have been obtained, it is a simple step to determine which have been passed. More important than that is finding out who has supported and who has opposed his bills. In addition to identifying local constituents supporting or opposing his actions, it is useful to contact statewide organizations affected by them. Thus, if a legislator has filed bills on conservation, it would be a good idea to contact not only the local ecology and hunting organizations but also the major statewide lobbying groups interested in conservation.

Any bill of significance has probably been analyzed by the special interest groups affected by it. A labor union, for example, would be a good source of information about a bill affecting wages or working conditions. A bill changing teacher certification procedures has undoubtedly been studied by teachers' associations, the state department of education, or an association of school administrators.

Whether or not the incumbent is running again, studying the incumbent's record is a convenient means of identifying areas of legislation to which a candidate ought to devote attention. He may find that the incumbent's legislative interests coincide very well with the district's needs and problems, in which case the challenger will have to work even harder on his own legislative proposals; or he may find that the incumbent is completely out of step with the district and is ignoring its problems. A review of a legislator's performance is a simple way of learning the requirements of drawing up and gathering support for legislation.

Sizing Up the Opposition

Sizing up an opponent's strengths and weaknesses is not the same as studying an office or the issues involved with it, although the two tasks overlap in the case of an incumbent. In addition to learning the opposition's public record it is also important to determine where his voting strength lies and who his most active supporters are.

A. Voting Strength

A detailed analysis of voting patterns in past elections is an essential tool for planning campaign strategy. Knowing which segments of the population vote most, how they usually vote, what issues bring them to the polls in greatest numbers, and who has voted for the opposition candidate in the past is of utmost importance. A careful study of voting patterns can easily help provide the margin of victory — by showing where campaign efforts should be concentrated.

To make a reliable analysis of voting patterns it is best to obtain records for a complete set of elections (rather than the results of just one race) and to compare the patterns in various years. These records should be available from local or state election officials.

Voting analysis is at best a risky business, since each of the variables involved is bound to change from one election to the next. Variables such as the number of registered voters can be fixed with certainty, but others, such as the importance of a given issue, are completely unmeasurable.

The simplest situation in which to analyze an opponent's strength would be the case of an incumbent in a district which has not changed in size or composition and in which there has been little population turnover since the last election.

We will assume that this is the case in discussing the patterns in the charts shown here.

Given: Oldfield is a working-class town dominated by conservative Democrats. Lakeview is an upper-middle-class area where independents are by far the largest class of voters, but which tends to be liberal and Republican. Milltown is a solidly Democratic middle-class area, and tends to be liberal.

Table One shows the latest population and registration figures available in 1972. Incumbent state representative John Linton of Oldfield, a conservative Democrat, ran for the first time in 1970, winning against liberal Eleanor Pitts of Lakeview in the primary and against Republican John Hodge of Lakeview in the final.

On the basis of this information and the accompanying charts, what important insights into voting patterns could be made by a Democratic candidate from Milltown who wanted to challenge Linton in 1972?

1. The first thing any prospective candidate should notice is that there are 6000 eligible voters in the district who have not bothered to register. Twelve hundred of these are in Milltown, our challenger's home, while 2300 more are in Lakeview, where Linton did poorly in both of the 1970 races. Both

Table 1
1972 Figures

	Total Pop.	Total Elig. Voters	Total Reg. Voters	Reg. Dem.	Reg. Rep.	Reg. Ind.
Milltown	10,000	6,000	4,800	2,700	500	1,600
Lakeview	15,000	8,500	6,200	1,500	1,900	2,800
Oldfield	20,000	13,500	11,000	4,000	2,100	4,900
Total District	45,000	28,000	22,000	8,200	4,500	9,300

Table 2
1970 Democratic Primary

	Linton	% Won	Pitts	% Won	Total Votes Cast	Per Cent of All Votes Cast
Milltown	525	55%	425	45%	950	35%
Lakeview	150	27%	400	73%	550	20%
Oldfield	800	66%	400	33%	1,200	45%
Total District	1,475	55%	1,225	45%	2,700	

Table 3
1970 General Election

	Linton (D)	% Won	Hodge (R)	% Won	Total Votes Cast	Per Cent of All Votes Cast
Milltown	2,400	60%	1,600	40%	4,000	24%
Lakeview	1,600	35%	2,900	65%	4,500	27%
Oldfield	5,000	63%	3,000	37%	8,000	49%
Total District	9,000	54%	7,500	46%	16,500	

of these groups represent potential sources of strength against Linton.

The same is true of the district's 9300 independents, some of whom might be persuaded to register as Democrats in order to vote for a liberal from Milltown running against Linton.

Since Linton won the last primary by only 250 votes, it would not take a major registration effort to bring in enough new voters to cancel out that margin. (We are assuming for the moment that the challenger could keep all of the votes that went to Pitts in the last primary.)

2. Half of the registered Democrats are in Oldfield, which is Linton's home. Whatever else his strategy, no newcomer could afford to ignore Oldfield. In order to beat Linton, it would be necessary to do at least as well there as Pitts did, and then to do better than Pitts did in the other two towns.

3. Milltown was an especially important factor in the last primary and probably would be in any primary, since its Democrats register and vote far out of proportion to the size of the town. A Milltown Democrat could thus expect strong backing.

4. Lakeview contains a heavy anti-Linton or anti-Oldfield vote. Linton lost badly in Lakeview in both of his past elections. The fact that Pitts did well is a favorable sign for a challenger to Linton.

5. Oldfield Democrats turned out in very poor strength in the last primary, while those in Lakeview and Milltown turned out well. It would be to the challenger's advantage to have the Oldfield voters stay home again in 1972 while increasing the turnout in both of the other towns.

6. The winner of the Democratic primary is virtually assured of winning the final election, on the basis of registration figures at least. The primary is therefore the place to fight hardest.

Putting this all together in the form of a strategy, the challenger would be wise to start his campaign early, concentrating on registering new Democrats in Milltown and Lakeview. He would also want to bring out as high a primary turnout as possible in both towns.

At the same time, he would have to campaign hard in Oldfield in order to prevent Linton from picking up the former Pitts voters. It would not be a good idea to attempt a heavy registration drive in Oldfield, however, since new voters there would be apt to go to Linton more often than to anyone else. Similarly, it would probably not be worthwhile to encourage a high voter turnout in Oldfield.

The analysis provided above is elementary but still useful. Far more detailed breakdowns of various statistics could be made — particularly if data on housing patterns, voter age, income, occupation, or other factors were included.

It is important to be cautious about relying on numbers. It is essential to be aware of the issues that played a part in the election results under analysis. The analyst should ask why Linton was so popular in Oldfield, for example. Was it merely because he grew up there, or was it because of an issue in Oldfield on which Pitts took the wrong stand? Could the Republican Hodge have done better if he had more financial resources, or was his performance unusually good for a Republican in this district? What were the voting patterns in 1968 and 1964, both presidential election years? The answers to questions such as these are as important as the purely arithmetical indices contained in election statistics.

While making an accurate voter analysis might seem to be more trouble than it is worth, the important point to keep in mind is that the purpose of such an analysis is not prediction but information-gathering. For example, if it is found that the voter turnout in a certain precinct has not been more than 40 per cent for the past eight years, that is a valuable piece of information. A candidate must then attempt to learn why this

pattern exists. Is it because voter registration has been discouraged there? Is it because politicians have never taken the
trouble to campaign in that precinct? A candidate discovering
such a pattern would need to account for it in his campaign
strategy. A candidate who found that a certain precinct had
never in its history elected a member of his party might want
to make an extra effort to overcome party sentiment in that
precinct or might decide to ignore it entirely. Voter analysis is
a means of learning how voters have behaved in the past,
rather than of trying to predict how they will behave in the future. The candidate's goal in using the analysis is to understand the past well enough to plan properly for the future.

B. The Opponent's Supporters

Knowing who an opponent's most important supporters are
is just as valuable as knowing who has voted for him in the
past. Either type of knowledge makes it possible to begin
planning ways to chip away at his strength and take advantage of his weaknesses.

In the case of an opponent who has been in previous contests, it may be possible to obtain a full record of his financial
support. Records of political contributions should be on file
with local or state election officials. A check on the records of
contributions to all local candidates in the recent past might
reveal who an opponent's political allies are. (Many candidates conceal some contributions, so that it is not always possible to get a complete record.)

In addition to learning who one's opponent's financial backers are, it can also be useful to find out what clubs, religious
groups, professional associations, and other organizations he is
affiliated with. The support a politician gets is in part an indication of where he will stand on a given issue, and can often be
turned directly against him.

If gun control legislation were an issue in a campaign, it

would be helpful for a candidate favoring gun control to know that his opponent was a member of the National Rifle Association. If there were a black community in the district it would be valuable to learn that one's opponent was a member of a racist organization. If one's opponent were opposing a tenants' rights organization, it would be helpful to learn that he had received campaign contributions in the past from a slumlord. Knowing an opponent's friends is thus as important as knowing his enemies.

Position Papers and Initial Strategy

Once the initial research on the job, the issues, and the opponent has been done, it becomes possible to start mapping out strategy for the campaign and to develop positions on particular issues. What will be the major campaign issues? What are your opponent's shortcomings and how can they be revealed? What do you have to offer as an alternative? The answers to such questions will depend as much on a candidate's personality and style as on the objective conditions surrounding the campaign.

Of course, very few candidates have the good fortune to determine exactly what the battles will be, and when and where they will be fought. It would be naive to expect that a tentative strategy drawn up early in the campaign would not have to be revised considerably before election day.

A candidate can line up his basic issues and begin developing programs early. These can then be made the subject of a series of position papers, campaign newsletters, and other campaign literature. A few important position papers should be ready by the time a candidate announces, since they provide a convenient center of discussion in press conferences and releases, in meetings with groups of voters, and in contacting possible supporters.

A position paper does not need to be a scholarly work and it certainly does not need to be "objective." However, it should be based on accurate information and should be articulate. Even on complex matters, a position paper probably should not be longer than about 1000 words, since few voters will read even that much. Most important, it should be able to stand on its own merits. Finally, it should be written in clear and simple language.

A candidate must avoid locking himself into an overly detailed position on an issue where new information might require that he change particulars. It is necessary to retain some surprises for the latter part of the campaign. Position papers can be fed to the press gradually at different times, so that each paper has its own chance to get publicity.

Community Contacts and Exposure

One part of the early strategy of any campaign should be to make the candidate well known in the community before his candidacy is announced. There are numerous ways for an unannounced candidate to meet people, gather support, and attract publicity before making his announcement. The more visibility a candidate develops by using these methods before declaring his candidacy, the more credibility he will have as a candidate.

Community organizations of any kind can serve the vital purpose of introducing a prospective candidate to community leaders and a wide variety of citizens. Any organization — athletic, fraternal, social, ethnic — constitutes a subgroup of the community which has its own interests, problems, and perspective. Joining or taking part in the activities of such organizations is a good means of making contacts and gaining understanding of local thinking.

Taking part in another person's campaign is also a means of

learning political techniques and problems and of meeting the politically active members of a community.

One of the best ways for a prospective candidate to build up his visibility is speaking before local audiences. There are usually a wide variety of organizations in any community which are in need of speakers to liven up their meetings. Lions and Kiwanis clubs, church groups and women's clubs and other organizations can serve as forums for any candidate to make himself and his views known. (A candidate who has not announced should not take advantage of a nonpolitical invitation by responding with a campaign speech.)

All it should take to begin a series of speeches is an introduction to one group and a good performance. Since organizational memberships normally overlap, it should be possible to arrange a second appearance elsewhere by meeting members of one group who also belong to a second group.

There is no need for a candidate to wait until after his announcement to put forth his proposals for legislation, new programs, or new policies. In fact, the chances for an unannounced candidate to get attention and publicity for his ideas are probably better than they are for a declared candidate.

Besides forming the basis of articles, letters to editors, and speeches, the ideas a candidate develops in his research and preparation of position papers can also be presented directly to the government agencies concerned. In many states it is possible for any citizen to file legislation on his own initiative. In places where that is not possible, the unannounced candidate could send his proposal to a local legislator and simultaneously issue a press release to gain public credit.

Proposals on purely local problems can be taken directly to the public official or board in whose jurisdiction they fall, again with the issuance of press releases. For example, a candidate concerned about drug abuse could bring a proposal to a school committee or police chief. If the proposal is to be made at a public board meeting, the local press should be informed in time to be able to cover the event.

Letters to the editor columns, radio and television talk shows, and other public access media outlets should also be exploited to the full by an unannounced candidate. (Letters to the editor rank among the most read sections of any newspaper and very few editors reject articulate letters.) Press releases are helpful in gaining news coverage, but they should not be regarded as the only way of using the media.

Weekly newspapers and small dailies are seldom able to pay enough salary to obtain good writers. Editors of small papers are often more than happy to have full-length articles contributed for publication.

Assessing Campaign Resources

By the time any candidate makes his announcement, he should have a fairly detailed estimate of how much money and manpower he needs to complete his campaign. While he almost certainly will not know where he is going to get everything, he should know what he intends to spend on advertising, how many volunteers he will need, where his headquarters will be, and so on.

For a brief race in a small community, these resources might not need to be very great. In a campaign that will last three or four months in a district with 15,000 or 20,000 voters, the need will be large.

In scheduling campaign expenditures it is essential to remember that it is much easier to cut back on expenditures at the beginning of a campaign than at the end. (It might not be a major setback to open campaign headquarters a month late, but it would be utterly disastrous to have to close it a month early.) Since almost any expenditure will seem worthwhile two or three weeks before election day, this early planning is also a good protection against one's own enthusiasm. Finally, it is sometimes essential to be able to show potential contributors a detailed campaign budget in order to justify a request for funds.

What applies to money applies equally to manpower. Finding and recruiting capable campaign workers is a lot easier for a candidate who knows whom he needs well before he needs them. This is particularly true in light of the fact that most experienced political workers will have committed themselves to some candidate well before the campaign season arrives. A candidate who waits until the last minute to do his recruiting may find the right number of people but discover that the talented or experienced people in the community are already working for somebody else.

Final Preparations

The final stage in the preannouncement period is to bring together enough resources to be able to put the campaign on its feet and to discuss the campaign with anyone who may be a source of support or who ought to be informed in advance of the announcement.

By the time any candidate who has done extensive preparation makes his announcement, it may not be surprising to the more knowledgeable members of a community. Politicians, party officials, newspaper personnel, the candidate's friends and acquaintances and other individuals may all very well know about a candidate's plans before he makes an official announcement. For a variety of reasons, however, each of these categories of people should be informed of the candidate's intentions before a general announcement is made. Party officials should be informed and consulted, partly out of common courtesy and partly because their advice or support may be needed. The same is true of other politicians, including even the opposition candidate.

It is also good policy for a candidate to visit newspaper editors or reporters and local television or radio station managers prior to making an announcement, also as a matter of courtesy. The last week before making an announcement, a candidate should pay a call on editors, explain why he is running and ask the editors their opinions on the campaign and the issues. (In other words, give the editor a chance to deliver his first editorial about you in person.) An editor will usually keep the information confidential temporarily if asked to do so, and will appreciate a candidate's consideration in letting him be the first to know about the campaign.

Finally, any candidate should certainly inform all of his friends and potential sympathizers before making a public announcement. Calling people up and asking for their support and advice before making an announcement is a good way of showing trust in them and increasing the likelihood of their active support later. Besides, anyone who really is the candidate's friend shouldn't have to learn about his campaign through the newspaper.

Making an Announcement

For a great many local candidates, the announcement of candidacy is the single most publicized event in the campaign. That being the case, an announcement should be staged to have maximum impact. (Among other things, this means that an announcement should not be made on the day of a moon landing or presidential address.) The less credibility a candidate has, the more of a need there is to see that his announcement is noticed by the public. A candidate with low credibility needs all the publicity he can get in order to have his name recognized by the voters; the process of reaching the public should start on the day the announcement is made. This can be done by planning a mailing or leafleting drive to coincide with the formal announcement, by calling a press conference, by staging a rally, or by other means.

In addition to being a formal notice to the public, the announcement is also a convenient focal point around which to organize the campaign itself. For example, if a direct mailing to voters were made on the day of the announcement, it would require both money and manpower to conduct the mailing. In planning for his announcement, the candidate can lay the foundation of the campaign organization by bringing together contributors and volunteers for the mailing.

Regardless of how the announcement is made — at a dinner, on a radio advertisement, or in a press release — the important point is that an announcement should not be a declaration that someone *will* run for office, but a statement that he *is* running. It should mean that he *already* has the resources to wage a serious campaign.

It should be clear that preparing a campaign is not a simple matter, at least if the work is done thoroughly. It might appear that the recommendations in this chapter are overly cautious or demanding. But every bit of preparation a candidate does should eventually be of value.

The precampaign period can involve as much as a year's effort for an important office in a large district. Even to run for a school board seat in a small town it could take several months to prepare an effective campaign.

Political campaigns can be put together hurriedly and with far less care than suggested here. But a candidate who is serious about winning owes it to himself to be well-prepared and he owes it to his supporters to be serious. A candidate who has not done the groundwork for his campaign will regret it when the going gets rough at the peak of the campaign. A candidate who is clearly well-prepared also may gain an edge in his campaign by scaring away other prospective candidates who consequently decide not to run.

3

The Organization

OF ALL THE RESOURCES needed for any political campaign, manpower is at once the easiest to obtain and the easiest to squander. A popular candidate who knows how to organize people — or who has a campaign manager who does — should be able to compensate for much of what he lacks in money with skillful use of people. A good campaign can be run on a shoestring budget if the right caliber and quantity of volunteer labor is assembled. Even the most expensive campaign is only as good as the staff behind it.

The key word is organize. A campaign work force will not spring up spontaneously at the sound of a candidate's name. Nor will any amount of manpower have the desired effect without proper leadership. Nothing is more pathetic than a group of volunteers working for a cause without knowing where to direct their energy. It requires hard-working and sensitive leaders to mobilize a volunteer campaign staff.

Size

Campaign organizations vary in size from the group of three or four people trying to get a friend elected in a small town to the casts of thousands working in any presidential campaign. But whatever the size or complexity of a campaign organization, its basic tasks are the same. Organizations of different size differ mainly in how much division of labor there is among staff members. The more workers there are, the more need there is to separate various tasks and to delegate responsibility.

In discussing the numerous jobs that exist within any campaign organization, we are not assuming that every local campaign will have dozens of specialists to draw upon. Many local organizations will have no full-time personnel. In others there may be several full-time volunteers working for months before the election. In one case, the candidate himself will be campaign manager, press secretary, and fund-raising chairman simultaneously, while in others he will have separate staff members filling each of these posts.

Whatever the size of a campaign, it is necessary to make some distinction between the different levels of commitment of various workers — as with the difference between paid staff, full-time volunteers, and part-time workers. It is also important to take into account that some tasks require constant day-to-day attention from one individual, press relations being a good example. Other jobs, such as phoning volunteers for a leaflet drive, lend themselves to constant substitution of one worker for another. In the course of this chapter we shall discuss the full range of campaign jobs, indicating ways of streamlining the organization and differentiating staff functions.

The Candidate

Because there is only one candidate in any campaign, his time and energy must be used where it has the greatest impact: among the voters. As much as possible, the candidate should limit his involvement in the internal affairs of the campaign organization to work that absolutely requires his presence. For the most part, this limits his role to decision-making on policy matters and passing judgment on campaign programs affecting the public, such as the distribution of campaign literature.

In a small campaign it is quite possible that the candidate will end up taking part in routine tasks such as stuffing envelopes or supervising canvassers. This type of activity should be strenuously avoided by a candidate, however. The more time he spends in the obscurity of headquarters, the less personal contact with the public he will have.

It is a common pitfall among inexperienced candidates to get caught up in trivial work such as typing letters or helping to copy voter registration lists. Either because he is nervous about going out on the street and meeting people, or because he doesn't quite know what to do, a new candidate may dive into any type of campaign work that makes him feel busy. A candidate who does this may work sixteen hours a day and never get to see anyone but his volunteers, which is hardly the way to become known to the electorate.

In jobs such as stuffing envelopes the candidate's role should be nothing more than symbolic. If fifteen volunteers come in to stuff envelopes at night it is a good idea for the candidate to be there to get the work started (as when the ancient emperors of China used to shovel the first spadeful of soil to start the spring planting). Once the job is begun, however, the candidate ought to be on his way out the door to deliver a speech or knock on doors. Candidates should have better things to do than stuff envelopes.

The Campaign Manager

The choice of a campaign manager is the single most important decision a candidate makes. The manager's responsibility can be described as making it possible for the candidate to go about his own job without having to wonder whether his organization is being run properly. It is the campaign manager's job to see that everything that needs to be done is done well and on time, thus leaving the candidate free to worry about issues, attend various campaign events, and maximize his time with the public. If the candidate and his manager have a relationship of trust, the candidate will be able to go about his business without having to worry about whether advertisements have been purchased, neighborhoods have been canvassed, or the campaign is heading for bankruptcy.

The campaign manager's role is the most varied and comprehensive in the organization: he assembles volunteer work groups, schedules events, oversees public relations efforts, and bears ultimate responsibility for anything done in the candidate's name.

While the candidate and the manager may share the most critical decisions, it seems to be the consensus of political experts that as much decision-making power as possible should be given the campaign manager. The reasoning behind this is that the candidate himself too often loses the objectivity necessary for making important decisions. The importance of the errors a candidate sees are magnified by his emotional stake in the campaign, while his optimism is fed by the reluctance of friends to give him bad news. Also, of course, the candidate is liable to know less about the details of running the organization than the manager should know.

In a large campaign the campaign manager's many responsibilities may keep him from being involved very deeply in any one task. Instead his job will be to consult with various workers, to trouble-shoot in particular crises, to set priorities and to assign responsibility for individual jobs.

Finance Committee

One group of workers that can easily be separated from the main branch of the campaign organization is the fund-raising or finance committee. Because of the type of people it is desirable to have on a finance committee, they may not be involved in the daily affairs of the campaign. These should be people who have either donated substantial amounts of money to the campaign or had experience in fund-raising or related financial activities.

Members of the finance committee should above all be people whose judgment would be respected by potential contributors — successful businessmen or executives, members of boards of schools or colleges, or people with similar experience. Any candidate should try to locate people who have been involved in other local fund-raising efforts — such as drives to pay for a hospital, support a charitable foundation, or finance a political organization. The members of the finance committee should know before they begin where money is likely to be found in the community.

Aside from the fact that members of the finance committee may be people too busy to work in the campaign itself, there is a second reason for separating them from the organization to some extent. Anyone contributing a large amount of money to a candidate is likely to have strong or extreme political opinions. As a result, there is a tendency for the fund-raising committee to put pressure on the candidate whenever a large contribution is in the offing. A candidate thus must be wary of pressure being applied to him by the finance committee. If the finance committee is insulated from having too much contact with the candidate or the rest of the organization, it is easier for the candidate to avoid the committee's influence.

(The same principle applies with the volunteers, who also tend to have strong or extreme views. Any candidate must learn to fend off the pressure applied on him by his supporters, who may pressure him to adopt their views as his own as the price of support.)

It is sometimes useful to permit some members of the

finance committee to be members in name only. A well-
known doctor who has contributed substantially to the campaign might not need to do any actual soliciting of funds in
order to attract support for the candidate by being listed as a
member of the finance committee. A finance committee
which exists in name only is not going to raise much money,
however. Someone on the committee has to be doing a lot of
work.

Not all fund-raising efforts need to be handled by the
finance committee exclusively, of course. Mail, advertisements, dinners, and other fund-raising chores can be executed
by the general campaign staff. But the finance committee's
job is to plan and coordinate these efforts and to see that
money keeps flowing into the campaign.

The crucial point about any fund-raising effort is that the
size of a contribution often depends on who is asking for it.
Whoever approaches a potential contributor should be as close
as possible to the contributor's income bracket and social class.
(The finance committee should be selected with that thought
in mind.)

Communications

Press relations and the preparation of advertising and campaign literature are activities that by nature belong under the
control of the same arm of the organization. The work of the
communications section of the staff will include: personal contact with reporters and editors, analysis of press coverage, writing press releases, designing campaign literature and advertisements, and photographic work.

Because of the importance of mass media in any modern
campaign, it is invaluable to have professional assistance in
these areas. A candidate should try to recruit volunteers with
backgrounds in journalism, advertising, photography, and

graphic design. Every campaign uses press releases and advertisements, both efforts in which amateurism is likely to be
costly. (An experienced graphic artist might shave hundreds
of dollars off the cost of a single printing job.)

If the candidate himself is not solely responsible for press relations, the responsibility of his press secretary and other workers should be carefully spelled out. The last thing a candidate
wants is to have various campaign workers freely volunteering
inaccurate or damaging information to the press. On the
other hand, there should always be someone available to give
information to the press when it is needed.

The main reason for unifying communications functions
under one arm of the organization is that it is important to
have a coordinated approach to the various media. The content of press releases, advertisements, and campaign literature
should be consistent. If the same staff members handle all
three, the campaign's public statements will be consistent, and
it will be easier to build a particular image. (Since all forms of
public relations are based on repetition of a message, a campaign's communications program should all be working to get
the same message to the public — and use essentially the same
facts, figures, and vocabulary in each attempt to get the message across.) To have the advertising staff working separately
from the press relations staff would be to risk having different
or even conflicting public images of the candidate.

Research

Even the smallest campaign has use for an active research
group working on jobs such as developing position papers,
writing speeches, compiling voter lists, or conducting polls.

Because much research work is highly specialized, volunteers doing research can often operate independently of the
campaign organization. Also, since most research jobs do not

involve contact with the public, those who are shy or unwilling to work with the public often find research work appealing.

For example, a position paper on the need for a local flood control project might be written by an engineer willing to work for the candidate but unwilling to take part in other activities. He need not have anything to do with the campaign except to turn in his report.

In a task such as conducting an opinion poll, it is sometimes convenient or even necessary to have the work group separated from the campaign. A survey on campaign issues will yield more reliable results, for example, if the people doing it are not identified with a candidate.

Other research functions include analyzing the opponent's campaign, compiling studies of the voting population, and preparing maps and lists for the use of other workers. The research section is a campaign's think tank, working behind the scenes and not itself attempting to affect the public.

Treasurer

As in any organization, the treasurer is responsible for keeping a tight rein on all funds flowing into and out of the campaign treasury and thus staving off financial chaos. Except in a very large organization, the treasurer can also assume the functions of accountant and purchasing agent and still not have a full-time job.

In conjunction with the finance committee, it is the treasurer's job to see that all contributions find their way into the treasury. A related and equally important job for the treasurer is to see that contributions are all recorded and reported in accordance with state law.

The treasurer's most important function is to see that the organization's spending is done only according to schedule and only for authorized purposes. As much as possible, the treasurer should have personal responsibility for approving every expenditure in advance. There is a great danger in allowing authority to spend money to be dispersed. If each staff member is allowed to spend what he thinks is necessary for his job, he will probably spend more than he should. After all, anyone in any organization tends to think of his job as slightly more important than anyone else's.

Field Operations

By far the largest and most complex group in any campaign is the field operations group, consisting of a wide variety of workers ranging from the regular headquarters staff to participants in periodic efforts such as leafleting drives. The field operations staff, by nature, frequently increases in size and then shrinks again, according to what kind of work is being done.

Since the most important requirement of this group's leadership is the ability to bring together large numbers of people to work quickly and efficiently, it should be headed by the campaign's best organizers.

The field operations group's responsibilities include:

1. Staffing headquarters — which means at least seeing that someone is always on hand to answer the phone, obtain supplies, and prepare for coming events.

2. Setting up precinct organizations. In an area where there are more than a handful of precincts, the organization must have special representatives in each precinct. The activities of precinct leaders should be planned and coordinated by headquarters staff.

3. Organizing special events. Coffee hours, rallies, dinners, and other such affairs must be carried out by volunteers working in conjunction with headquarters staff.

4. Leaflet drives and canvasses. Large numbers of volunteers must be recruited and trained for special efforts such as these.

5. Telephone polls and surveys.

6. Voter registration.

7. Processing data. Large groups are needed for tasks such as transcribing information from voter lists to file cards.

8. Addressing envelopes. Whenever a mailing is planned, numerous workers are needed to address and stuff envelopes.

The field operations group's activities, in short, account for most of the man-hours in the campaign and most of the organization's direct contact with voters. Besides being the largest campaign work force, it thus also needs to be the best.

Election Day Group

Of all the challenges facing the campaign organization, making sure that voters sympathetic to the candidate get to the polls is the most critical. Since polls usually are not open for more than about twelve hours, it is vital that campaign workers getting out the vote be well-prepared for their jobs. Organizing election day workers well in advance and as a separate task force is a good means of insuring its success against the hectic pace of the last few days before the election.

Organizing them well before election day makes it possible to weed out anyone who will not perform well.

Four to six weeks before the election, an election day task force should be organized and taught their jobs. While everyone working on election day may already have been involved in the campaign and working in a specific group, it still is best to set up a clearly defined staff as the election day task force.

Recruiting an Organization

As large and complex as it may seem, the organization described above is a good model for a local campaign of any size.

No candidate can have too many people working for him — provided that each worker has something to do and does it in a way that brings credit to the candidate.

What an organization is, as opposed to what it can be, depends on how diligently the candidate works at building it. Bringing together the people necessary to mount an effective campaign is a difficult challenge. Nevertheless, any candidate who starts early and has something to offer to his community should not be faced with an insuperable task in recruiting an organization.

A campaign organization does not need to grow up overnight. The seeds of an organization are sown in the precampaign period when the candidate starts calling on friends for advice and assistance. By the time he announces his candidacy, he should have gathered together a core of supporters, including probably his campaign manager, someone to staff an office, a finance committee chairman, and a few persons interested in occasional volunteer work.

Starting with a nucleus of this sort, it should be possible to draw increasingly wider circles of people into the campaign as they are needed. This is not to say that they will all spontaneously volunteer. Very few people just volunteer to take part in a campaign. They have to be asked. It may take several requests to fill each campaign job slot, but the only way to recruit volunteers is to ask for help from anyone who expresses an interest in the campaign.

There is a great reluctance on the part of inexperienced candidates to ask people for help. Similarly, most people who have not taken part in campaigns are hesitant to volunteer — since they may know nothing about political campaigning, they assume that they could not be of any help to a candidate. That is all the more reason for a candidate to be perfectly blunt and not hesitate to say he needs help. If they are not asked, most people are liable to assume that they are not needed.

Adding Links to the Chain

Once the growth of an organization has begun, it can be made to proceed geometrically — simply by having each recruit bring in two or three friends as the need for them arises. As soon as a volunteer is personally committed to a campaign, he can be easily persuaded to bring along a friend to help out in the next job that needs to be done. The more momentum and publicity a campaign develops, the more people become interested in taking part in it.

A good example of the way in which a narrowly based organization can be turned into a community-wide effort is the method by which a chain of neighborhood receptions linking different segments of the community can be organized. In planning a coffee hour in a neighborhood where he knows people, the candidate can arrange to have a few strangers from other neighborhoods invited. With the cooperation of his host at the first reception, the candidate can then arrange to have one or more of the people from the other neighborhoods hold a reception. In like manner, section after section of the community can be penetrated, until there are no longer any areas where the candidate does not have committed supporters. The same principle can be applied to any phase of a campaign.

In addition to neighborhoods, every community is divided into numerous other overlapping subgroups: club memberships, church congregations, school attendance districts, groups of people who shop in the same place or who live in similar types of housing. Each of these subgroups can be made a target of the campaign, and can be used as means of meeting still further subgroups. (For example, if a candidate meets a PTA official at a coffee hour, he can seek introduction to a PTA meeting. If he then meets a doctor at the PTA meeting, he can ask the doctor for introduction to local medical organizations.)

Ultimately, a campaign should be represented by volunteers from every possible subgroup of the community, so that each voter can be personally contacted by someone he knows. This is especially important in the case of residential blocks, so that on election day each voter can be contacted by a neighbor.

The vast majority of people willing to take part in a campaign are housewives or students. These seem to be the only sizeable population groups with enough time to devote to campaigning and enough sense of responsibility to be willing to do the difficult work required. A campaign should make a determined effort to attract other categories of workers as well.

Put Everyone to Work

A fundamental principle regarding the use of volunteers is that no one should be asked to join a campaign until there is something for him to do. On the other hand, no one who volunteers should be turned away.

When volunteers get the impression that they are not really needed, they begin dropping out of a campaign in boredom or disgust. It is hard to bring such people back when they are needed. (What is worse, word of their experience is liable to reach other would-be volunteers and prevent them from offering their services.)

Anyone who offers to work should either be given something to do or told exactly when he will be needed. It is hard to imagine having to refuse help. An extra volunteer can always be asked to pass out leaflets somewhere or to help canvass a neighborhood.

Since it is good practice to keep a file on all available volunteers, anyone who offers to work should be asked to leave his name, address, and phone number and to indicate when he could work and what type of work he would be willing to do. If a volunteer cannot be used immediately, someone in the organization should write or phone him to show that he is still remembered and will eventually be wanted.

Although it is bad to turn away assistance, it is better to do so than to have a lot of people standing around headquarters doing nothing and possibly demoralizing those who are working.

Quality Control

One of the most critical jobs a candidate must handle personally is to set and insist upon standards of excellence for all campaign activities. In large part this means setting standards for the selection and performance of volunteers.

In order to maintain a high performance level, it is necessary to some extent to screen out volunteers who do not work well, who cause friction or are otherwise more of a liability than an asset. This does not mean there needs to be a formal evaluation procedure. It does mean that whoever is supervising a group of volunteers should know who is doing a good job and who isn't. A telephone canvasser with a sharp tongue, for example, is going to do more harm than good for a campaign. Anyone who starts turning off voters or is not working well should be reassigned or removed from the campaign entirely. On the positive side, anyone whose performance is particularly good should also be singled out for greater responsibility.

"Be Clean for Gene" became a slogan of the McCarthy campaign of 1968 with good reason. The candidate and his staff should lay down firm guidelines as to what is acceptable dress, hair length, or behavior for volunteers who meet the public. Voters tend to identify a candidate with the people who represent him. It's up to the candidate himself to say who he wants representing him.

Job Assignments

Wherever possible, it is best to try to match a volunteer with a job that fits his time, talent, and interests. Obviously, it is not possible to carry this principle too far. The basic work for which volunteers are needed consists of tasks such as handing out leaflets, addressing mail, and interviewing voters. Nevertheless, there is enough variety in the types of work to be done for some choice to be permitted. No volunteer should be given a choice between one specific job and no job at all.

An equally important point is that job assignments should always be well-defined and of limited duration. A volunteer should not be swamped with a load of work far beyond what he said he was willing to do. The job should be small enough to be done well in a limited time, but still challenging enough to make him feel that he is accomplishing something. In no case should a volunteer be given vague instructions such as "mind the shop," or left to his own devices to figure out what needs to be done.

Finally, anyone deserves to know why the job he is doing needs to be done. The more boring and repetitive the job is, the more this is so. The reason for doing any job ought to be known to any volunteer involved in it. A candidate can play a useful role in providing motivation to workers doing rote tasks by showing his personal appreciation.

Training

Training is not done very much in political campaigns, perhaps because it always seems that there is no time for it. Most political volunteers are asked to do things they have never done before, however, and they should be instructed carefully on how to do their jobs. A little attention to training prevents a lot of wasted time and low quality of work.

For volunteers who work with the public, for example, role-playing is a good training technique. A volunteer who will be doing door-to-door canvassing will benefit immediately from having different people act out the reactions he is likely to get from voters.

Whenever possible, campaign staff should prepare written instructions governing the procedures to be used in various jobs. In all cases a volunteer should be told exactly whom to contact for help or advice. A supervisor or experienced staff member should always be available to help out volunteers who run into difficulty.

The use of standardized procedures makes it possible to substitute one worker for another without major hitches. It is also best to subdivide any task into as many smaller jobs as possible. This makes it possible to involve more people in any one assignment at the same time. (Stuffing, addressing, and stamping envelopes is a good example of a job where it would be more efficient to have three people at work instead of one).

Scheduling and Coordination

Any time a group effort is planned, it is essential to see that the people and the materials needed are all brought together at the same time. If twenty people are asked to come to headquarters at 7:00 p.m. to stuff envelopes, then someone had better see that the door is open and the necessary materials are on hand. Poor planning or unnecessary delay in such a situation can only lead to hard feelings on the part of people who took the trouble to show up on time. The logistics of working with large groups requires great foresight. If a group of volunteers is to be driven to various places to hand out leaflets, the volunteers, their leaflets and instructions, and their rides need to be coordinated, so that no one is left standing on a streetcorner for an hour with nothing to do.

Gratitude

The fact that people are not getting paid for their work in a campaign makes it all the more necessary to demonstrate that their efforts are indeed appreciated. A great many successful politicians pay so little attention to their volunteers that it is a wonder they attract any workers. The volunteer is the most important person in a campaign organization, aside from the candidate, and should be treated as such.

Volunteers should be treated to refreshments during or after their work when particularly difficult tasks are completed. More important, a volunteer should always be personally thanked by someone whose attention will matter to him (if not by the candidate, then at least by someone high enough in the organization to show that someone up there is thinking about the volunteers). A phone call or a written thank-you note from headquarters is a minimum display of appreciation.

Another way of showing respect for volunteers is to see that their working conditions are as pleasant as possible. There should be a conscious effort to see that work areas are kept clean and comfortable. When routine work is being done, providing a radio or phonograph is a good way of picking up morale and making the work go easier.

The Organization as Community

Mounting a political campaign is a process with extremely important human aspects, completely unlike the process of bringing together workers in an office or assembly plant just to get a job done.

Many of the people who get involved in a campaign do so because a campaign headquarters is a low-risk place to meet people, a place where they can join a new group and make friends without making an overt effort to do so. In addition to their political ideals and their thoughts about the candidate, they bring with them a need to be joined together in some common purpose and to develop new bonds with their community.

A campaign can be a perfect outlet for the unexpressed emotions people carry about inside them — the need to feel that they are doing something that matters, the desire to exert some control over the world around them, or merely the need to escape from the loneliness or the monotony of their normal lives.

The emotional content of a campaign is the reason for many of the excesses of campaigning that are criticized by reformers. Political rallies, parades, and conventions are dominated by songs, balloons, and other expressions of gaiety not because of the cynicism of politicians but because these events are social events as much as anything else.

Part of the art of campaigning, therefore, is to take the social and emotional aspects of politics into account and to turn them to good advantage. People come into campaigns seeking a sense of community they cannot find elsewhere and it is in the best interests of a candidate to see that a sense of community is built.

In order for people to develop the bonds that together amount to a feeling of community, it is necessary for them to struggle together, to share both work and joy in pursuit of a common goal. A candidate who is able to bring people together in this emotional sense, as well as just to get the work of campaigning done, is tapping much deeper needs than those involved in arguing issues or introducing new ideas into political affairs. In the long run, the organization he has created will continue to live a life of its own well after he has been judged at the polls.

4

The Budget

MONEY IS FAR LESS a factor in a local race than it is in statewide or Federal races. Though any candidate must spend
some money on his campaign, there are innumerable ways in
which a lack of money can be offset by proper use of campaign
workers and campaign techniques.

How much money is needed to mount a winning campaign
depends not just on how large a district is or how much the opposition is spending, but also on how well a candidate is able
to use volunteer workers, and how much material he can obtain through donations of space and equipment. A small
budget can be converted from a liability to an asset if it forces
a candidate to focus on involving large numbers of people in
his campaign instead of relying on expensive media techniques
to reach the voter.

If letters are hand-delivered to every voter by campaign
workers, for example, more than a savings in postage results:
each worker has an opportunity to convey his respect and enthusiasm for the candidate to the voters he meets. The message the voter thus receives is perhaps much more important
than the content of the leaflet itself. Similarly, a successful
public relations effort can be staged by volunteers at little cost,
bringing as much favorable publicity as an opponent's high-
priced advertisements.

In any campaign, there is inevitably a certain point where it is impossible to cut back further on campaign expenses. Where that point lies, however, depends on the candidate's imagination and persuasiveness.

As will be shown in this chapter and the next, most of the usual campaign expenses can be either eliminated or trimmed down considerably, and there are many ways of raising funds that go unexplored by the majority of candidates.

The budget items included here are not to be regarded as necessities. Each item is included as a factor any candidate should take into account in calculating his budget even if it is eventually rejected.

Drawing up a campaign budget is a tricky business, since it is impossible to plan for every eventuality. A candidate who is the victim of an unexpected smear in the week before the election might be forced to pour everything he has into a series of last minute advertisements. Failure to mobilize enough volunteers might make it necessary to pay to have envelopes for mailing addressed by machine.

Even without such emergencies, it is rarely possible for a candidate to know how much money he can raise, and it is therefore difficult to plan a budget precisely.

Any candidate is likely to end up spending more than he can really afford and more than he originally planned. But that makes it all the more important to plan a budget carefully. Even if it is not possible to be completely accurate, it is better to end up being wrong by 10 per cent instead of by 50 per cent. The process of formulating a budget also is a means of establishing priorities, which in turn affect other aspects of campaign planning.

Once a budget is drawn up, it should be continually re-evaluated and revised in the light of experience. If there is any question during the planning stage as to what certain items will cost, it is far better to err on the generous side rather than be short of funds late in the campaign. It is never a problem to find a way to spend a few hundred dollars in the last week of a campaign, but it may be impossible to come up with that much in contributions at the last minute.

Personal Expenses

The first expense to be taken into account is the immediate increase in the candidate's own cost of living that will result from being a candidate. Everyday expenses such as laundry, baby-sitting fees, cab fare, telephone bills, and food and drink are bound to be greater for a candidate.

The candidate who intends to campaign full time for even a few weeks also must regard what he will give up in salary as a campaign expense. This is true even if the reduction in earnings is simply the result of refusing overtime pay.

Other likely out-of-pocket expenses include subscriptions to newspapers and periodicals, and fees for joining organizations to which he might want to belong, such as the Jaycees, Americans for Democratic Action, Civil Liberties Union, or the Sierra Club.

These personal expenses (to which might be added the cost of new clothing) probably would not be apparent immediately, but they must be included in the cost of running for office.

Staff Salaries

Very few local candidates have the money to hire full-time staff members, and in many campaigns it is not necessary to do so. Nevertheless, it is extremely important to have at least a few people who can give their full attention to running the campaign. In a large campaign it is essential to have a nucleus of people who stay with the campaign from start to finish, simply in order to give the campaign continuity and

The Campaign Budget

Salaries
    regular staff
    per diem assistance
Office expenses
    site
    equipment
        desks, chairs, etc.
        typewriters, cabinets, etc.
        telephones
        printing machine
        paper and other supplies
Subscriptions
    periodicals
    government documents
Printing
Postage
Transportation
Advertising
    television
    radio
    newspaper
    other outlets
Special events
Election day
    advertising
    mailing
    victory party
    other paraphernalia
Photography

stability. For this reason, a candidate without friends able to support themselves for two or three months while working for him might be forced to pay salary to someone.

If a decision is made to hire one or more staff members, however, the hiring should be done with the campaign's greatest needs in mind. For many candidates it might be better to spend $100 a week on a versatile secretary capable of running a campaign headquarters than to spend the same money on a campaign manager. On the other hand, if both a secretary and a manager are available as volunteers, money available for salary might best be spent on an experienced press secretary.

No one should be hired who would not otherwise be interested in the campaign. It would be better to make do with a part-time volunteer than to hire a staff member whose enthusiasm or loyalty is based primarily on his paycheck.

Considering how brief most campaigns are, it would also be foolish to hire someone who is not known to be qualified for his job. By the time it becomes apparent that a staff member is unreliable or incompetent, it will most likely to be too late to find a replacement. If someone must be hired, it should be the right person.

In granting a salary to any campaign worker, it is also necessary to take into account the effect it will have on other campaign staff members who are not paid. If both paid and unpaid people are working full time, it should be clear to everyone why one person is paid and another is not. A person drawing salary should be an obvious asset to a campaign. If he is not holding up his end of the work load, unpaid staff will have good reason to grumble.

In addition to regular campaign workers, it is also necessary to consider the possibility of hiring specialists on a per diem basis. A lawyer, accountant, or artist may have to be called in to work on problems which cannot be handled by volunteers immediately available. Careful planning should eliminate most such expenses, since volunteer workers with almost any skill can be found in the average community.

A final word about expenditures on staff is that anyone on a campaign payroll is likely to be looked upon by outsiders as a reflection of the candidate's standards. Contributors to a campaign like to think their money is well spent, and they will often judge the wisdom of their investments by the type of people the candidate decides to hire.

Office Space

In a small campaign, a candidate may be able to use his living room, cellar, or garage as a campaign headquarters. In other cases, it may be necessary to go to some expense to rent a place where volunteers will be able to work.

Even where rental space is essential, there is no need to spend a great deal of money to get an attractive office. If free office space cannot be found, then the cheapest available storefront should be obtained. With a bit of painting and sweeping, and the addition of posters, maps, and other decoration, almost any site can be turned into a comfortable and presentable headquarters. A paint-up, fix-up party at headquarters can be an excellent occasion for getting volunteers acquainted.

The main point to consider in choosing a headquarters site is what purposes it must serve. This means thinking about how much space is required for campaign workers as well as whether the site will be used for rallies, large meetings, or entertainment. It is also necessary to consider whether headquarters should be located in a place where it will attract public attention. An office on the third floor of a run-down building might provide an ideal work area at just the right price. It would not get the attention from passers-by that a ground floor site on a busy street would get.

It would be shortsighted to take a lease on a small office in June if a large number of workers were expected to be on hand in September. On the other hand, there is no sense in renting a large area that will be filled only on three or four occasions.

Whatever the space needs of a campaign, a site should be lined up well enough in advance to guarantee that it is available when needed and to permit early planning for office equipment and telephones. (Telephone installations should be requested early to avoid disastrous delay.)

Equipment

With the exception of telephones, it is often possible to beg, borrow, or create most of the material needed to run an office. In cases where rental equipment is considered, a close check on the savings involved in rental should be made. For example, it would make no sense to rent a typewriter for four months at $15 a month if one could be purchased for $80 and resold for $60.

Desks, tables, and chairs should be obtained for free, or else made as cheaply as possible. Even if no one has desks to loan, a perfectly useable work surface can be made with materials from a lumberyard. An old door with a flat surface, mounted on a pair of sawhorses, makes a fine all-purpose table.

Typewriters, filing cabinets, lamps, and similar items should be obtained through loans or donations.

Standard office supplies are needed in quantity. However, there is no sense spending large sums on high-quality paper for use within the office.

One of the most important assets of a well-equipped campaign office is a printing machine — whether a spirit duplicator, mimeograph, or Xerox. Such a machine is useful for reproducing instructions to campaign workers. For internal campaign purposes, it is best to use the cheapest possible means of reproducing printed matter.

If an office machine is used to print material to be sent out to voters, care should be taken in choosing the machine. Duplicating machines vary enormously in quality and versatility. There are also a wide variety of options available in telephone service. As is the case with office space, the need for telephones varies immensely in the course of a campaign, rising sharply when large-scale activities are underway. One way of saving on telephone expenses is to have volunteers do as much telephone work as possible at home.

In any location such as a campaign headquarters, where there are large numbers of strangers around, an unwatched telephone can be an expensive item. In order to avoid having people make unauthorized long-distance calls, it is a good idea to make one person responsible for keeping an eye on the telephone at all times. (Locks for telephones are also available.)

Subscriptions

A small part of the budget should be set aside for periodicals, documents, and other publications that may be needed by campaign staff. This includes not only subscriptions to all local news media, but also bulletins and magazines from unions, community organizations, and other groups whose activities the candidate should be aware of.

Printing

Printing is usually the largest single expense for a candidate for local office. Because of the great variation in the quality of different types of printed matter, no candidate should spend a large sum on printing without consulting an expert. The American public has conditioned itself to ignore even the best-designed advertisements, and it is impossible to attract attention with a low-quality leaflet in some areas. On the other hand, there are also sections of the public who are turned off by expensive brochures (which give the impression that a candidate has wealthy and powerful backers).

Commercially printed literature of the type normally used in political campaigns varies in price from less than a penny to eight or nine cents per unit. Quantity, reproduction method, the type of paper, and color scheme are only a few of the factors that affect the price per unit in a printing job. Only an expert can combine these factors to get the best product for a given cost. Getting bids from a variety of printers will also lead to considerable savings.

Since a delay in delivery can upset the schedule for a mailing or leaflet drive, a check with a printer's other customers should be made to see how reliable he is.

A candidate should think twice before sending printing work to a nonunion shop. The union emblem is normally affixed on political literature and its absence can be a liability. (Of course, it is more expensive to use a union printer.)

Postage

Postage is primarily an aspect of the printing budget, and can be as great an expense as printing. Since large portions of campaign literature can be delivered by volunteers, the postage budget is still separate. Considerable postage also may be needed for general headquarters purposes.

Postage is a much easier expense to calculate than printing. Once a decision is made as to what type of postage is to be used, the total cost of a mailing is a matter of simple multiplication. Each of the options for postage has its merits:

1. Stamps are the best form of postage for sending material to voters, since the presence of a stamp indicates that there is a personal touch in the mailing. A hand-addressed, stamped envelope is far more likely to be opened and read than any other type of political mail, with the exception of post cards. (One

experienced political worker claims that commemorative stamps get a better response than regular eight-cent stamps.)

Stamps are expensive, however, and the decision to use stamps for greater effectiveness in a mailing must be weighed against the cost. For fund-raising mailings or for mailings to limited groups of voters, it might be practical to use stamps. For a large general mailing it may be too expensive to use stamps.

2. Postcards are less expensive than letters or mailed leaflets, but should generally be used only for following up some other contact with a voter (e.g., reminding him to register to vote after a canvasser has learned that he is unregistered.)

3. Bulk mailing is the cheapest method of sending out campaign literature. On the other hand, third class mail must be handled according to precise postal regulations which limit its usefulness.

The main disadvantage of bulk mail is that it tends to be regarded as "junk," which means that much of the expense of a bulk mailing is liable to be wasted money. Delivery of third class mail is also erratic.

4. Business reply permits. Whenever the voter is asked to respond to mail he is sent, it ought to be as easy as possible for him to respond. A self-addressed, postage-paid card or envelope should be included in a mailing packet whenever feasible. Where large quantities of return mail are not expected, it is normally cheaper to use a business reply permit than to use stamps on the return envelope.

The advantage of using business reply cards or envelopes is that postage must be paid only for those which are *returned*. For example, if 1000 business reply envelopes are sent out and only 100 are returned, the cost to the sender is $10 (10 cents per returned unit under current regulations.) If all 1000 return envelopes had been stamped with eight-cent stamps, the cost would have been $80. Use of the business reply permit in this case would yield a savings of $70. Using stamps for business reply purposes makes sense only when the rate of return is expected to be very high or the cost of printing special envelopes is greater than the postage savings.

5. A wide variety of postage and addressing machines are available for rent or purchase. These vary tremendously in cost, from a small office meter intended for limited use which can be rented for a few dollars a month to large commercial machines which attach an address label to each piece.

This discussion of postage options is not at all complete. Any candidate planning on a large postal budget should consult his local postmaster, as well as a printer, for detailed information on regulations, the cost of bulk mailing, use of machines, and the cost of business reply permits.

Transportation

One possible transportation expense for a local candidate is the rental or purchase of a minibus or panel truck to carry materials or to shuttle volunteers around in peak work periods. Such a vehicle might also be used as a sound truck. The best way to meet this need would be to recruit someone with a vehicle to work in the campaign.

Advertising

The size of the campaign's advertising budget is likely to be closely related to the size of the printing budget, since what is done in one area helps determine what needs to be done in the other. As with printing, the advice of an expert (advertising executive or copywriter) is virtually a necessity to making the best use of money allotted to advertising.

The first step in arriving at an advertising budget is to list the local media in which ads might be purchased and to determine the relative importance of each one: daily and weekly newspapers, radio and television stations, and other outlets such as shoppers' guides, billboards, or window displays. The advice of local businessmen and other politicians can be valuable in deciding which of the various possibilities deserves most attention.

A. Television

Television stations usually cover such wide areas that their advertising rates put ads beyond the reach of most local candidates. This is not true everywhere, however, and cable television may bring lower rates and increased opportunity for local candidates to use television in their campaigns. In any case, it is worthwhile to inquire about a station's advertising rates if it gives good coverage of the voting district.

Television advertising is an art in itself, and expert assistance is more valuable in making television ads than in any other aspect of a campaign.

B. Radio

Radio advertisements are within the reach of most candidates, especially in a small community with coverage by a station with a strong local following. Aside from rates, probably the most important factor to keep in mind in deciding how much to spend on radio ads is how many people listen to the station at a given time, *and* who these people are. Many radio stations have detailed analyses of their listening audiences and this information should be available from a station's advertising manager. Beyond that, the characteristics of the audience differ from program to program. Advertising time should be planned and purchased with the size and nature of each audience in mind. In addition to using common sense and obtaining information from station personnel, it is also a good idea to ask a station's regular advertisers for their opinions on the choice of advertising time.

Radio advertising differs from television advertising in that it is much easier for an amateur to use effectively.

C. Newspapers

For most candidates in local campaigns, advertising primarily means newspaper advertising. Newspaper advertising rates depend mainly on the size and location of an ad within the paper and on the size of the paper's circulation.

Any newspaper's advertising manager should be able to provide precise information on who his paper's readers are and where they live, particularly if the paper has a high percentage of home delivery. By obtaining data on the circulation of various newspapers in an area, it is possible to aim advertisements at target groups of voters with almost as much accuracy as through a direct mailing.

Just as radio or television ads should be planned with a view to what programs they will interrupt, newspaper ads should be purchased on specific pages of a paper. An ad on page one or on the editorial page has much more impact than one placed in an obscure corner of the paper.

Another factor to consider in purchasing advertisements is the editorial policy of the paper or radio or television station. The type of coverage given to a candidate should be an important factor in his decision to buy an advertisement in a given outlet. Similarly, a candidate who visits an advertising manager to ask about rates should let the manager come to his own conclusions as to how much advertising he is liable to purchase. Some newspapers and stations become more generous in news coverage of a candidate if they think he is about to buy a lot of advertisements. There's no sense disillusioning an entrepreneuring editor.

D. Billboards and Other Signs

Billboards, window displays, signs on buses and cars, bumper stickers, and lawn signs are also effective means of advertising — at least to the extent of making a candidate's name well known, which in itself is sometimes a major task. A candidate using billboards should be sensitive to the location and environmental impact of billboards. Wall posters, similarly, should not be pasted up indiscriminately. Signs on the front lawns of supporters are a cheap and especially effective means of advertising.

Special Events

Any special event is liable to cost money. From news conferences to rallies, from coffee hours to testimonial dinners, there are an unlimited variety of events that can be staged to benefit a candidate.

What these events will cost and how many there will be depend entirely on the style of the campaign. The possibilities are limited mainly by the imagination and energy of campaign staff, since any event can be made to pay for itself.

Election Day

Just as the election day staff should be organized as a separate unit in the campaign work force, the budget for election day should be set aside early in the campaign. Then, whatever else goes wrong with the overall budget, there will still be the right amount of money left over for election day.

The major expense on election day may well be a final mailing to voters or a last-minute series of advertisements. In addition, the election day budget should include materials such as sample ballots, refreshments for volunteers, transportation for voters, tags to hang on doorknobs (reminding people to vote), and paraphernalia such as hats or lapel buttons. Finally, the election day budget should definitely include enough money for a victory party!

Photography

The services of a photographer are practically essential in most campaigns. There are enough amateur photographers around so that it should be no problem for any candidate to have photography done for free or at the cost of the materials. Nevertheless, it is mandatory that the photographer be fast-working enough to be able to meet deadlines (such as when a press release is being sent out to a morning paper after an evening event). In addition to being able to develop his own prints, he should be familiar with the needs of engravers and printers. A Polaroid is a valuable and practical piece of equipment to keep on hand throughout a campaign.

The list of expenses presented here is not a list of necessities. It is a checklist to indicate what the possible expenses are. With the exception of commercial printing, postage, and advertising, most of the items listed can be obtained for free or improvised by campaign staff.

The constant question for any candidate to ask about his budget is: "Is this expense really necessary?" A hard-nosed treasurer and an imaginative campaign manager are irreplaceable assets in running a low-cost campaign. There are numerous means of substituting volunteer labor for expensive machinery or outside services.

Any candidate should also be wary of the pressure to spend money which will be brought to bear on him by his own supporters, by the opposition's successes, and by salesmen and hucksters who try to convince him that some expensive gimmick is the key to victory. While a candidate's friends are trying to talk him into buying another $1000 worth of ads, there is liable to be a novelty dealer waiting in the next office to show him some autographed emery boards or other gadgets which frantic candidates often blow good money on.

Because campaigning has increasingly been characterized by big spending, very few citizens without wealthy backers even consider entering politics. The higher up the political ladder you look, the more this is true. But even on the local level it is not uncommon for candidates to rely primarily on expensive advertising. It is less and less common for people without money to run for office. In the remainder of this book, the emphasis will be on campaign techniques which use a lot of people and little money. Money is a necessity for running a campaign, but not to the extent that is widely believed.

As a last resort, any candidate truly strapped for funds can always turn necessity into a virtue, publicly declare that he is setting an upper limit to his budget and make campaign spending an issue in his race.

5

Fund-Raising

THE FUNDAMENTAL FACT about political fund-raising is that the only way for a candidate to get the money he needs is to ask for it — and to keep on asking.

No candidate can afford to be bashful about asking for support — financial, material, or otherwise. Any candidate who hesitates to ask people for money, ought to reflect on the fact that he is asking the electorate to give him a lot more than a few dollars — he is asking them to trust him with their government.

The proper attitude toward fund-raising is that a donation of money is the least that a true supporter should be willing to give to a campaign.

Confidence

No matter how determined a candidate or his fund-raisers are, no citizen is going to part with his money unless he has confidence in the person requesting it. The more of a bond there is between the person requesting a contribution and the potential contributor, the more likely it is that a contribution will be forthcoming. This means that every effort should be made to see that there is some kind of tie between the solicitor and the contributor. The connection between the two may be that they are neighbors, that they are in the same income bracket, or that they work for the same company. Whatever the case, a fund-raiser with something in common with the people he asks for money is likely to have far more success than one seeking money from a stranger or from someone from a totally different background. The contributor should have some specific reason to trust the solicitor, since it is impossible for most contributors to get a chance to learn to trust a candidate.

This is one reason why fund-raising by mail is relatively ineffective. A voter whose only connection with a candidate is a mass-produced leaflet or brochure has to be pretty dedicated to his political ideals to be willing to respond with a check. Very few voters know much about any candidate, so it is not surprising that they respond weakly to mailed appeals for funds.

A Contribution Is an Investment

No candidate should spurn the opportunity to obtain even the smallest contribution. Any donation is an investment in a candidate on the part of the contributor. Even a one dollar contribution signifies that one more vote is committed.

A contributor becomes personally involved in the campaign as soon as he makes his donation. Having given money, he is also likely to give other support to the candidate by telling friends of his investment and by encouraging others to vote for the candidate. In light of this, a candidate should be glad to have supporters hitting the streets to sell buttons, bumper stickers, and other campaign material. Not only does each sale raise a few cents, but it signifies the involvement of one more citizen in the campaign.

Contributions in Kind

Contributions in kind are to be just as avidly sought as contributions of cash or labor. Not everyone is willing to give money to a campaign and no one should be *limited* to giving money.

In fact, some people prefer to give a contribution *in kind* that in the end amounts to more than they would have given in cash.

For example, a couple who might balk at the thought of contributing $25 in cash may be persuaded to throw a cocktail party for a candidate. They may end up contributing far more than $25, and they will have the sense of having accomplished something and they will have involved others in the campaign as well.

The principle is true of both large and small contributors. The motives of such people are legitimate, and their instincts provide exactly what a campaign needs — the direct participation of people in political life.

To reiterate, anyone asked to contribute to a campaign should be given as many options as possible: it should be up to the contributor to decide what he has to offer. The more options a potential contributor is given, the more likely it is that he will contribute.

Fund-raisers should be sensitive to a potential contributor's preferences and not get hung up on seeking money alone — materials, services, and labor are just as much needed as money in most campaigns.

Know the Law

For his own sake and for the sake of his contributors, a candidate and his fund-raisers should know state and Federal laws regarding campaign contributions.

A candidate should see that neither he nor his contributors unwittingly violate laws regarding political contributions. Public employees are commonly prohibited from making political contributions, for example, as are corporations. In some states there are limits to the amount of money a candidate can spend or how much he can raise through one campaign committee. In others, as under Federal law, all political contributors must be identified by name, address, and occupation.

There are constant ethical questions that arise in political fund-raising as a result of the loopholes in such laws. For example, when public employees are forbidden to make political contributions, it is common for their contributions to be made in the names of their relatives. Where there is a limit on how much an individual can contribute, the same tactic is used. There is a great temptation to be all too willing to work around the law through such dodges. If his conscience is not enough to keep a candidate honest, he should keep in mind that if he circumvents the law, it makes it more difficult for him to criticize other politicians for doing so.

Information on campaign finance laws and other election laws can be obtained from the League of Women Voters in many states, as well as from state or local election officials. It is also a good idea to consult a tax lawyer or other expert to see that nothing in the law has been overlooked.

Avoid Embarrassing Contributors

As eager as he may be for funds, every candidate must be careful about where his money comes from. Most political contributors make donations in good faith, but there are also many who are looking for some favor in return.

A candidate should be at least slightly suspicious about unexpectedly large donations. He should not hesitate to return a check from someone who seems likely to expect a quid pro quo — such as a store owner worried about his liquor license or a contractor who frequently bids on public construction projects. Even if a candidate has no intention of making good on implied requests for favors, he is liable to regret accepting funds from questionable sources. For example, if a contributor is later charged with bribing one public official, the fact that he contributed to two or three other officials is liable to bring their names into the case even if they are innocent. It pays to know why any large contribution is being made.

The same applies to completely honest contributions coming from people who expect a candidate to grind their favorite axes, or from people with whom a candidate does not want to be associated. The price of one contributor's donation may be an understanding that a candidate should vote the contributor's sentiments on an issue such as sex education, while another may expect him to oppose a tax reform proposal. When a candidate and his contributors agree on an issue, there is nothing unusual about this type of understanding. When a candidate begins to permit his vote to be bought, however, he should rethink his reasons for getting into politics. Does he just want to get elected? Or does he want to win and serve on the basis of what he himself believes? It can be remarkably easy for a candidate to acquire contributions with strings attached, but it can also be embarrassing.

Accounting and Acknowledgments

Every cent contributed to a campaign should be accounted for, which means that the campaign treasurer should be the recipient of all funds. No money should be permitted to dribble into unauthorized hands, even if it is spent for legitimate purposes. There are several reasons why this is important.

First, any contributor has a right to be disturbed to learn that his money is not being properly used. The slightest indication of financial mismanagement in a campaign can be enough to scare off possible contributors and undermine confidence in a candidate.

Second, it is the job of the treasurer alone to decide when money is to be spent on any given item (in consultation with the candidate or his manager, of course). No one should have a chance to spend campaign funds without the campaign manager and the treasurer's advance approval.

Third, contributions can be reported only if they are recorded, which is again the job of the treasurer. Even if the law does not require all contributions to be recorded, records of contributions should be kept for the benefit of both a candidate and his contributors. (Completely apart from legal requirements, a card file on all contributors should be kept for future reference — perhaps for the next campaign, perhaps for a last minute appeal in the present campaign.)

Fourth, every contribution should be immediately acknowledged. Whether the contribution consists of a $100 check or three hours of volunteer work, anyone who contributes to a campaign should be thanked for his trouble. This can be done with a visit to the contributor, a phone call, or simply the candidate's signature on a note. A candidate short on gratitude should not be surprised if contributors are short on funds the next time he calls on them.

As a final note on accounting, all contributors should be encouraged to use checks or money orders, partly as a safeguard on the money itself, but also because it gives them permanent receipts for their donations.

When to Start Raising Funds

One of the lamentable truths about political fund-raising is that money is least available when it is most needed. Contributions typically peak in the last weeks of a campaign, long after the candidate has had to make key decisions about his budget. Accordingly, it is easiest to raise money in the last stages of a campaign — when the public suddenly realizes that there is an election coming up.

"Never say die" is therefore the watchword in fund-raising. Fund-raising efforts should be stepped up as much as feasible in the final stages of a campaign.

Since money is needed most *before* it is available, fund-raising efforts should begin as early as possible. Even if an early start does not bring a large flow of early contributions, it may cause late contributors to send their checks a crucial bit sooner than they otherwise would have. A general mailing at the time of the announcement is a good means of preparing people for later soliciting while also getting publicity early.

Finally, the tendency of funds to come in late also means that a candidate is often sorely tempted to take loans against the expectation that he will raise enough funds to pay them back. While it is fairly reasonable for a candidate who is doing well to assume that more money will be coming in, financing a campaign on loans amounts to betting on the behavior of the public. A candidate should be loath to take out a loan, and any candidate who does so should weigh his bet as carefully as possible.

Where to Begin

There is no better place for a candidate to begin raising funds than among his own friends and supporters. Starting with people they know, fund-raisers can work outward through the community to new sources of funds. Anyone willing to give money himself may be able to find a friend or two who might also contribute.

Another source of potential contributors is in the campaign contribution reports of incumbent officeholders and previous candidates. (These reports are public record in most areas and should be on file with state or local officials.) Besides the records of other local politicians, it can be even more profitable to check the reports of candidates for statewide and national office. Obtaining and examining all of these lists may be a lot of work, but the names on them are likely to be the names of the best prospects in the community.

If a fund-raising committee is well chosen, it should be composed of people who may have access to the fund-raising lists of other community organizations such as churches or private clubs, which are also good starting points.

The Personal Approach

The person to person appeal is by far the most productive means of fund-raising, and the closer the tie between solicitor and contributor, the greater the likelihood of a contribution.

Though any number of campaign workers may eventually be drawn into fund-raising efforts, the process must begin with the candidate himself, when he begins asking for money and help to launch the campaign. As the effort broadens, the candidate may play a smaller and smaller part in making requests to individuals. Nevertheless, he should always be on call for occasions when a promising prospect seems to require an introduction before writing a check.

Committees

When the candidate and his friends have exhausted fund-raising sources among people they know, it then becomes necessary to begin devising ways to reach strangers. One effective means of reaching new sources is the use of committees composed of people belonging to various community subgroups: Teachers for Jones, Lawyers for Jones, West Side Committee for Jones, etc. The range of possible committees is virtually unlimited. Anyone known to be respected by his peers can be made the chairman of a committee of his own creation and sent out to hunt for committee members, donations, and more new contacts for the campaign. (It goes without saying that anyone permitted to raise funds in a candidate's name should be a person who will be an asset to him. Anyone who isn't likely to command the respect of the people to whom he is speaking should be put to work only in some activity where he can do more good than harm.)

Door to Door Appeals

As a rule, door to door fund-raising drives are poor sources of political funds. If a resident of a neighborhood is asking friends on his street to make contributions, a door to door drive may be successful. When the solicitor is a total stranger to the people he is asking for funds, he is not likely to have much success.

A door to door drive should never be the first campaign effort conducted in a neighborhood, since first impressions do stick. It's not a good idea for the voter to have a better memory of having been asked for money than of being told who the candidate is. A door to door drive might be made after a general canvass has screened out sympathetic and unsympathetic voters, but not to a totally indiscriminate selection of voters. Once again the solicitor should not be a complete stranger to the neighborhood.

Considering the energy required to conduct any door to door canvass, it is probably best to concentrate the time of canvassers on more productive efforts.

Sales of Campaign Material

One brand of fund-raising in which anyone can take part, and which is still personal, is the sale of campaign paraphernalia such as stickers, posters, buttons, pens, and ties. The sale of these goods may not produce startling amounts of revenue but they do give volunteers something to do and they put the candidate's name before the public. Such materials can easily pay for themselves.

Buttons and other such materials also make volunteers readily identifiable as campaign workers and they give workers a convenient means of introducing themselves to strangers. Finally, any voter who walks away having purchased a sticker or button identifies himself with the campaign more conspicuously than if he had simply read and thrown away a leaflet.

Mail and Leaflet Appeals

Given the relationship between personal contact and fund-raising success, appeals for funds made by mail or by leaflet should not be expected to be terribly profitable. For that reason, no literature used for fund-raising should be designed to serve only that purpose.

Any printed matter distributed for fund-raising purposes should give the reader a variety of alternatives for action and should provide him with enough information so that he will want to act.

For example, if a letter advertising a fund-raising dinner is distributed, it should include a space (possibly on a return-addressed, postage-paid card) reading roughly as follows:

A. Enclosed please find my check for $____ for ____ tickets.
B. I cannot attend the dinner, but my contribution for $____ is enclosed.
C. I would like to a) ____ volunteer at headquarters, b) ____ assist in a neighborhood canvass, c) ____ take part in a voter registration drive.
D. I would like more information about the candidate. ____

Name _____

Address _____

Even if the recipient of such a letter does not send money, he may respond for other reasons. If he merely sends his name and a request for information, he identifies himself as being interested in the candidate and gives campaign workers a justification for following up on his interest in some way. For example, his name and address could be forwarded to a neighborhood volunteer who would then pay a visit to his home. No response from a voter should go unanswered, while the voter should be given every encouragement to respond in some way. Most importantly, the time and expense that it requires to put a piece of campaign literature in a voter's hand should be made as useful as possible by combining fund-raising efforts with other objectives such as publicity and information-gathering.

Because a *general* mailing is more effective for publicity purposes than for fund-raising, any attempt to obtain contributions by mail should be directed at *specific* target groups. The profitability of a mailing is likely to be directly proportionate to the number of people on the list who have made contributions to campaigns in the past, or who have already expressed sympathy for the candidate.

As much effort as possible should go into reducing the impersonality of mailed literature. The more individual effort it requires to send a piece of literature to a voter, the more impact it is likely to have. A handwritten note is almost certain to be read, if not answered, while a machine-addressed printed flier is more apt to be ignored. (There is no sense making half-hearted efforts at giving a personal touch to a piece of mail, however; no one will be fooled by a letter on which the voter's name and street address are handwritten while his town's name is preprinted.)

Even literature produced by machine can be individualized to some extent. A school committee candidate, for example, might send a different letter to parents of children in one school than he does to those of children in another. Any such subgroup — policemen, teachers, union members, businessmen — can be made the target of a specialized mailing which is more likely to be read than a general form letter. Special interest committees can be used to reinforce the reader's identification with a piece of mail as well; the names of a teachers' committee could be listed on the letterhead of a letter sent to teachers, for example. As with person to person fund-raising, any mailed appeal should establish as much rapport with the reader as possible before requesting money.

Advertising Appeals

The same general principles apply to advertising as to leaflets and other literature used for fund-raising: selection of a target group, the use of a coupon, and general publicity value are elements which should go into the making of any ad.

One of the best uses of advertising for fund-raising purposes is the signature advertisement — that is, an advertisement containing the names of a group of voters who have paid for the ad in order to show support for the candidate.

The basic principle on which the effectiveness of the signature ad is based is the same as the principle on which a great many local newspapers are run: people like to see their names and the names of their friends in print. If twenty-five people pay one dollar each to buy even a small ad, they are likely to have dozens more friends and relatives who will look at the ad. No matter how fine the type or how long the list, many readers will check every name to see who is supporting whom. Not only is such an ad tremendously effective, but it also does not cost the candidate a cent.

The signature ad is a variation on the committee-sponsored ad, which can be run in the same way but without the names of all contributors listed. (Some people don't like to see their names in print.)

One important precaution should always be taken in signature ads, however: The consent of any contributor should be obtained in writing before his name is included in an advertisement. This can be done quickly and simply by having solicitors carry preprinted release forms on which the contribu-

tor need only sign his name and address. The contributor
should also see the content of the ad he is signing.

Failure to obtain such consent is liable to result in lawsuits
filed by contributors who did not quite understand what they
were doing when they made their contributions. Anytime
there is reason to doubt a contributor's identity, the worker
gathering signatures should check on it before the ad is
printed. (There is liable to be some practical joker who signs
another candidate's press secretary's name on a release form.)

Fund-Raising Events

Fund-raising is easiest when the person asked to make a contribution can be offered a direct return on his money, and the
perfect way of making fund-raising a two-way street is to hold
fund-raising events. Probably the most certain means of
making a fund-raising event a success is to make people *want*
to attend it whether they support the candidate or not. The
way to accomplish that is to see that the fund-raising event is
more of a social event than a political rally.

A campaign should hold at least one event which not only
raises money but which becomes the *major social event of the year*
in his community. That is a large order, but it is within the
reach of any candidate with supporters who are both ambitious and imaginative.

What type of event will serve that purpose is likely to be
different in every community. In a voting district on a harbor,
lake, or river, it might be a boat cruise for 200 or 300 people
— complete with dancing, food, and drink. In a college community it might be a rock concert. In a rural area it might be
a carnival, country fair, or picnic.

The important thing about any fund-raising event is that it
should tap the spirit of a community; it should bring residents
of a neighborhood or a district together in a congenial setting

and in a way that they do not usually have a chance to meet. Among the myriad of possibilities for such events are: meals of all kinds — bean suppers, spaghetti suppers, barbecues, pot luck dinners, buffet luncheons, wienie roasts, specialties such as Chinese food or shishkebab, and so on; dances; concerts — banjo, classical, rock, folk; movies — at homes or at a rented theater; plays or skits; auctions — of art, furniture, handicrafts, etc.

The uniqueness of such an event can also be a key to making it a fund-raising success. For example, if there is an historic or architecturally unique home in the community which very few local citizens have entered, people might be attracted to an event there just to get a look at the place. An evening of Laurel and Hardy movies in someone's backyard might well be too much for even the opposition's supporters to pass up.

No candidate should *start* his fund-raising events on a grandiose scale, since it takes time to gain experience in making events such as the above come off smoothly. Early in the campaign, fund-raising events might start on a modest level — cocktail parties, small dinners, and coffee hours. Moving upwards in scale from a small house party to a barbecue for seventy or eighty is a matter of improved coordination and planning. The size of the events to be held can grow in the same organic fashion as the campaign organization itself. (The details of planning large events will be discussed in the next chapter.)

A prerequisite to planning any fund-raising event is the designation of a specific target group the event is supposed to attract — whether that means teenagers, college students, couples, elderly people, or whole families. There is a specific market for any product, and an event is a product.

Finally, the cost of an event and the desired profit margin should both be carefully calculated, so that a minimum attendance level can be set. There is no sense going ahead with the planning of a fund-raising event if it cannot reasonably be expected to raise funds. If an event is not expected to make a profit, this should be understood from the outset.

The last point leads to a general principle pertinent to all fund-raising activities. There are some activities which earn money for a campaign, there are others which merely break even, and there are still others which inevitably cost money. The first and second type of activities serve fund-raising purposes; any event which breaks even monetarily has made a profit if it generates publicity and good will for the candidate. Any activity which loses money, however, should unquestionably be begun only if there is a particular purpose it will serve.

Campaign money and manpower should be spent on only those activities which are essential or beneficial to the campaign. While a campaign is not a profit-making enterprise, everything done in the campaign should be judged in cost-benefit terms. That is true above all of fund-raising activities.

6

Tactics

EVERYTHING DONE by a campaign organization — from fund-raising to licking stamps to passing out leaflets — has meaning only to the extent that it contributes to one or more of a campaign's three main objectives:

> Bringing favorable attention to the candidate and his views
>
> Identifying voters sympathetic to the candidate
>
> Bringing those voters to the polls

Research, advertising, writing press releases, and other activities contribute to attaining these goals. But the essence of any campaign is *person to person* contact between the candidate, his supporters, and the public.

Direct human contact is the most effective means of influencing the voter. This is especially so on the local level, where such contact can *be* the campaign. The various methods for achieving the above objectives — with people rather than through the use of media — are the subject of this chapter.

Community Involvement

The type of campaign we are most concerned with here operates on the principle of involving the community in the campaign as much as possible. Community involvement means a) getting as many people as possible to contribute to the campaign in some way; and b) "reaching" or "touching" each voter frequently.

The first aspect of a community involvement campaign has been mentioned already in previous chapters: every citizen who contributes to a campaign has an investment in it and thus has a personal stake in the fate of the candidate. Not only will he vote, but he is likely to be active in encouraging others to vote.

The second aspect, "touching" every voter, is the basis of all campaigns. Where the conventional modern campaign relies primarily on reaching voters through the media, a community involvement campaign tries to reach them through personal contact.

A community involvement campaign seeks to build up a network of committed supporters with roots in every segment of a community. The object of this effort is to fully identify a candidate with his community. The candidate and his workers must become involved in the activities and the concerns of his constituents. A candidate must consciously and actively reach into every corner of the community to mobilize this support. The campaign must reflect the broad needs and interests of as many elements of the community as possible.

Meeting the Voter

There is no better way for a candidate to establish a reputation, influence voters, and drum up support than to get out and *meet the public* at every available opportunity. On street corners, at factories, and door to door, a candidate should meet every voter he can.

A candidate meeting people on the street can hardly hope to present them with much of a discussion of issues, but even the briefest meeting serves legitimate purposes. It gains visibility for the candidate and it makes him known.

People generally do want to have face to face contact with a candidate — he becomes a human being in their minds, rather than an inaccessible or abstract creation of journalists and public relations men.

Meeting voters is a two-way process. A candidate will learn a great deal about his community by canvassing on foot and looking more closely at his district than he has ever done before.

Door to Door Tours

The surest way to reach every voter is to make a door to door tour of every street in the district. Any candidate in a district of less than 40,000 residents can hope to meet every voter in this way.

A candidate who does not systematically attempt to visit every household risks meeting only a narrow range of people. The people who attend most campaign events are likely either to be already favorable to the candidate or to be people who have a greater than normal interest in politics.

It may well take hundreds of hours of walking to completely cover even a modest-sized district in house to house visits. For a candidate who is campaigning full-time, this could mean weeks of walking, while a candidate who is doing it in the hours after work may have to spend months of evenings and weekends making door to door tours. The value of personal canvassing by a candidate cannot be overemphasized: it is one of the few techniques whose value candidates who have tried it almost unanimously agree upon.

Whether an entire district or only key areas of a large district are to be canvassed, the first step in making a door to door tour is to map out the area to be reached. A few days of walking are enough for a candidate to learn how much he can accomplish in a given time, and then he can set up a schedule for the whole campaign. Having established his pace, the candidate can map out the district in areas suitable for a morning or evening walk or for a full day's touring on Saturday or Sunday.

Here are a few tips:

1. Know exactly what streets you will cover on a given tour.

2. Make a map and keep a record of each area that has been covered.

3. It often helps to carry a list of residents along the route to be covered, correcting it as you go.

4. Determine what time of day is best for touring each neighborhood. People in different areas are home at different times. In most places it is unwise to campaign after dark.

5. Before setting out to tour an area, check on local problems and be prepared to discuss them (e.g., an overcrowded school or poor garbage collection).

6. Never have liquor on your breath. If offered a drink, refuse as politely as possible.

7. Carry a few dog biscuits, in case a dog or two start following you (dogs can't vote, but they can be quite a nuisance).

8. Practice a useful dialogue or approach that you feel comfortable with. (Role-playing with friends will reveal ways of dealing with hostile reactions.) Be sure to explain exactly who you are and what you are running for: you will find some voters who don't even realize there is an election coming up.

9. Always carry some item that you can leave behind with people — a card, leaflet, brochure — as a reminder of your visit.

10. Don't be overly persistent in ringing a doorbell even if it seems that someone is home. Two or three rings is enough. They may not want to be interrupted.

11. If no one answers, leave a card on the doorknob which

says "Sorry you weren't home when I stopped by." Since you have put a great deal of effort in getting to the door, you should not let that effort go to waste. A card or leaflet for this purpose can be preprinted.

12. Develop a means of winding up very long conversations. While it is a pleasure to find people who are interested enough to want to talk for a while, a series of long conversations with a few people will prevent you from reaching a far greater number of people who are not interested and whom you have to spend time on. For the same reason, it is best to avoid going into people's houses. If someone is interested in talking at length invite him to come to a coffee hour or some other campaign event.

13. If someone responds enthusiastically, seek some commitment from him. Invite him to a campaign event. Make notes on the positive reactions you receive and follow up your visit with a phone call or card, possibly asking the person to contribute to or take part in your campaign. If you do ask someone for help, don't put him on the spot: Make your request, but say you will telephone for an answer later. Don't be pushy.

14. If someone gives you a strongly negative reaction, you may want to note it and then see that his name is not on your mailing list.

A door to door tour is liable to be extremely discouraging at first, especially for an unknown candidate. It is not easy for a candidate to get used to the large number of indifferent or even hostile reactions he may receive.

It takes time to develop an approach which brings a good response from people. When a candidate knows he has several thousand homes to visit, the difficulty of the first few hundred may tempt him to abandon the door to door tour. He should realize that the reason why the tour is difficult is precisely that he is not known. Once a candidate begins to gain a reputation, voters begin to have more curiosity about him and it becomes more rewarding.

Other Meeting Places

In addition to door to door canvassing, there are numerous other opportunities for a candidate to meet voters: at shopping centers, factory entrances, sports grounds, and other public places.

Since many of the places where large numbers of people gather are centers of a specific activity (work, shopping, recreation), a candidate trying to meet people in such an area does well to just hand out leaflets, mention his name and the office he is seeking, and chat briefly with those few people who have the time to stop. A candidate should be aware that people are more likely to be hostile in public places than when they are at home.

The Coffee Hour

In addition to the brief meetings with people he has on the street, or at the door, it is essential to hold events which allow a candidate to have more extensive contact with voters. The best way to accomplish this is in a group of fifteen to thirty people in the relaxed atmosphere of someone's home. The occasion for such a meeting can be a cocktail party, beer break, or luncheon, but the cheapest and easiest event to get people to sponsor is the coffee hour.

Such gatherings can be held at any time of day, although it is important to remember that the time of day determines who is likely to be present. A morning coffee is likely to be a women's event, while it is easier to attract men or couples at night. Coffees can be the best way to campaign in the evening, after it is too dark to go out knocking on doors.

Instruction Sheet for Neighborhood Coffee

(to be given to hostesses)

1. Invite at least 30 couples. You can expect about half of them to show up. Invite people from your neighborhood and interested friends.
2. Make out two copies of the enclosed invitation list and return one copy as soon as possible. The other copy is yours.
3. We will send a note to all the people on the list, confirming the invitation.
4. Shortly before the coffee, call each guest to remind him of the event. This will significantly increase the number attending.
5. General format for the coffee:

    10 a.m. (or whatever time is scheduled)
        Guests arrive. Informal socializing.
    10:30 The candidate gives a brief talk.
    10:45 Questions and discussion.
    11:15 Coffee breaks up.

Note: This outline is simply to give you an idea what to expect. If you have any questions, please call_____

                          Thank you

(This illustration and others throughout the book are intended only as examples of what can be done, not as rigid models.)

The coffee hour is one of the most effective means for a candidate to learn an area's problems and to build up firm bases of support. The personal contact offered by such an event is worth any number of leaflets or advertisements. Not only do those attending have a chance to question the candidate and register their personal concerns with him, but the impressions they receive are likely to be much stronger and more valid than after any other type of contact with a candidate.

The coffee hour is a means of penetrating segments of the community where a candidate is not yet known. Each coffee hour can be used as a tool for recruiting sponsors of still others in new areas of the community.

To get a long chain of coffee hours underway, it is best to begin by holding one for a group of friends from various sections of the community. Each person present can be asked to duplicate the event in his own neighborhood. A candidate can go on meeting new people, locating more sponsors for these events, and reaching into areas increasingly further from his base of support. A candidate should make certain that he is meeting mostly new people at each event. It doesn't do much good to keep talking to the same people week after week.

There are a number of guidelines which should be followed in setting one up. For instance, as in all political events, nothing should be left to chance. A candidate and his workers should always assume that anything that can go wrong will go wrong. If a problem can be foreseen it should be dealt with in advance.

In choosing a host or hostess make sure that he or she is a person who is accepted in his or her neighborhood. A host who is something of an outcast in his neighborhood will not only have a hard time attracting guests but will also be identified with the candidate. The opposite is also true: a well-liked or respected host will reflect favorably on the candidate.

There should be some contact between the candidate and

the host (even if only a brief conversation) before he is asked to sponsor an event. Contact with the candidate will make the host more enthusiastic about holding the event and will also permit him to speak more authoritatively about him to the people he is inviting.

In arranging a series of coffees, it is useful to distribute a list of guidelines for each host to follow. There are also a number of general principles to observe in setting up coffees:

1. No more than two weeks' lead time should be allowed between the time a sponsor is asked to hold a coffee and the date it will be held.

2. Campaign staff should check with the host two or three times during that interval to see that all preparations are being made.

3. Host should be asked to submit the invitation list to headquarters at least a week in advance, so invitations can be sent out from headquarters.

4. Both written and telephone invitations should be made to each guest.

5. From one third to one half of invited guests can be expected to show up. If fifteen people are desired, thirty or forty should be invited.

Before going to a coffee hour, a candidate should be sure to learn about neighborhood problems. In addition to preparing a brief talk, he should be sensitive to problems such as dealing with low turnouts and closing off questions when they begin to be trivial or to go far afield of the campaign. He should be careful to bring an end to the event before it collapses of its own weight. Any candidate needs to explore different approaches in order to find one with which he is comfortable. A scenario for a typical coffee is for the candidate to arrive a bit after the guests, work his way around the room to meet people, and then give a talk. While the length appropriate to a coffee hour varies, an hour and a half is about the upper limit for keeping a group's attention.

The candidate should carry a notebook to take down the names of interested people and should write down questions he is unable to answer on the spot. Answers should then be sent out *immediately* after the event.

Every guest should have the opportunity to leave with a leaflet or button and should know where to obtain further information or to volunteer.

Before the candidate leaves, he should speak with the host about the type of follow-up that may be needed with various guests. He may ask him to sound some of them out about the possibility of holding coffee additional hours.

Large Social Events

There are advantages to large events that can outweigh the increased cost and the sacrifice of close contact with guests offered by events such as coffee hours. A dinner, picnic, or fair can be a major social event which will attract people who would not attend any other type of campaign activity. A large event can also be the occasion for a major fund-raising effort, a source of publicity to have an impact even on those who do not attend, or a means of attracting congressional or gubernatorial candidates.

The principles involved in planning a large event are the same as for a coffee hour, but there are far greater logistical problems: finding a suitable location, getting commitments from those expected to attend, planning meals, speeches, and other activities, and worrying about problems such as whether there is enough parking space and where each guest should sit. The larger an event, the more details there are to take care of and the greater potential there is for a disaster.

Staging a Rally

The problems involved in staging a rally illustrate many of the complications involved in any large event.

A rally can serve a number of purposes: building up campaign spirit among workers, demonstrating the solidarity of a group which supports a candidate, attracting publicity, and showing off a candidate beside other speakers who support him.

The key to holding a successful rally is not only in the planning as to what will take place or where it will be, but in guaranteeing that enough people show up to make the rally a success.

A site for a rally (and for most other events) should be much smaller than the "expected" attendance figure would call for. Any event looks less important than it is to the participants if it is held in a room which is half empty. An overflow crowd in even the smallest hall is likely to be enthusiastic, while the same group in a larger room would not feel its numbers to be impressive.

An outdoor rally should be held only at a place which can be made to look crowded even if it cannot be filled. A hundred people standing in the middle of a baseball field would not impress anyone, but the same group outside a small building might look like a mob. If a large open area must be used for a rally, surrounding the audience and the speaker's platform with a ring of cars and sound trucks is a means creating a sense of being closed in, and thus of bolstering the impression of crowdedness. A couple of bands, thirty or forty people with signs, and a hundred guests in such a situation would constitute a decent rally. Without the props, group spirit would be more difficult to stimulate.

A checklist of considerations in planning large events should include: parking facilities, entrances and exits, fire precautions

and fire regulations, police supervision, the availability of telephones, lighting, and a sound system, as well as plans for who
sits on the platform or at the head table. Managing a rally is a
job for an experienced master of ceremonies.

Jerry Bruno and Jeff Greenfield devoted a whole book,
The Advance Man, to the subject of planning major political events. Anyone planning an event for more than a few
hundred people should read it.

In regard to attendance, three figures should be kept in
mind: the capacity of the site, the size of the crowd desired,
and the size of the crowd likely to be achieved. Guaranteeing
that the right number of people show up requires more careful
planning than any other aspect of a rally.

Bringing a crowd together should be accomplished with as
much personal contact as possible, through telephoning and
leafletting if not in person. The person in charge of attendance should keep track of solid commitments to attend the
rally, so that an accurate estimate of attendance can be
made.

The Campaign Worker and the Public

No matter how hard a candidate works at meeting the public,
it is his campaign workers who will inevitably carry the real
load in gathering support on the individual level. There must
be constant emphasis on the need for each worker to favorably
influence as many voters as possible.

Gathering Nomination Signatures

In most places it is necessary for a candidate to obtain a
specified number of signatures of registered voters to place his
name on the ballot. When this is the case, the signature drive
provides a good opportunity for the mobilization of a campaign organization.

If only a small number of signatures is necessary to have his name placed on the ballot, a candidate's first inclination might be to gather only the necessary number, plus a few more as insurance against the invalidation of some signatures. (The number of signatures gathered should be double what is needed. Certification procedures are often so strict that large numbers of apparently valid signatures are voided. Many a candidate has been knocked out of a race because his nomination petitions did not have enough valid signatures.)

Rather than being limited to gathering the necessary number of signatures, a signature drive can be organized to be a major event. A large scale drive puts volunteers to work, reinforces their commitment to the campaign, *and* brings the candidate's name to the voters. If a major signature drive serves no other purpose, it at least serves as a dry run in which campaign workers can gain experience working together in preparation for more difficult tasks that lie ahead. Everyone who signs a petition should be sent campaign literature and asked to support the candidate in other ways.

As the sample instruction sheet for volunteers indicates, gathering signatures correctly requires care. There are usually precise specifications prescribed by law regarding nomination signatures. These requirements should be included on instruction sheets.

Leafleting

High on the list of basic activities in any campaign is leafleting — in neighborhoods, shopping centers, recreation areas, offices, factories, parking lots, or wherever large numbers of people are found.

Leafleting should not be done in a manner which is offensive. The aftereffects of a leaflet drive should not include littered lawns and streets, or voters irritated by overly aggressive leafleters.

Instructions for Circulating Nominating Petitions

We would like to have several thousand signatures on these petitions when placing the candidate's name on the ballot for the primary. The filing date for signature is _____, but we would like to have all petitions returned to headquarters by _____.

The petition drive is an excellent opportunity for bringing the campaign into all local areas. Any information you learn in talking with voters should be written down next to their names on the voter registration list with which you have been provided (e.g., party affiliation, sympathetic, refusal to sign petition). Please try to contact all persons eligible to sign the petition in your area.

Carry leaflets and bumper stickers with you and offer them to people who seem interested.

Note:

This petition may only be signed by _____ (check local law).

(Indicate other legal requirements for obtaining valid signatures, such as whether erasures are forbidden, how a signature must appear, whether pencil is permitted, etc.)

A leaflet drive, like a mailing or advertising campaign, can be set up with particular target groups of voters in mind — homeowners, parents, apartment dwellers, shoppers, commuters — and the leaflets can be designed with the target groups in mind. Though it is more expensive to have several different leaflets, the use of a single leaflet throughout a campaign should be avoided. People will not read the same leaflet twice.

While the leaflet is being prepared, plans for distribution at appropriate places can be made. Maps of the areas where the drive will take place should be included in volunteers' instruction kits. There are several other procedures that should be followed in any leaflet drive:

Determine how much manpower is available and make a schedule for the drive. Break down the workload into units small enough for each volunteer to complete on schedule.

Line up the necessary volunteers and have them attend a meeting to receive instructions and materials. Every worker should understand why his work is important and why it must be done according to plan. (The less interesting any job is, the more important it is that workers understand why it needs to be done.) If transportation is needed, it should be arranged at this time.

Give each volunteer a deadline for completing his job, and ask him to report when he is finished. Post a large map of the district on a wall at headquarters, and color in sections where the drive is finished. This is good for morale and is encouraging to volunteers who don't ordinarily see the big picture.

Decide on some debriefing procedure, i.e., some means of getting feedback from volunteers as to what response the leaflet brought, what special problems they encountered, and so on. This information can be useful in planning future activities.

Neighborhoods: Volunteers delivering leaflets to homes or apartments should be especially careful not to put leaflets in places where they will antagonize people: on their car windows, on lawns, or scattered around doorways.

Factories and office: It is easier to give leaflets to people entering work than it is to those leaving. They're in less of a hurry.

Streets: Tables can be set up for the benefit of leafleters working on a street. A table provides a center of attraction and eliminates the need to approach people.

Any leafleter working in a crowded area should pick a spot where he can stand still and people must come past him, instead of where he must walk up to each person in a crowd.

Leafleters should always wear a name tag, button, or other identifying device, so that they are easily identified as campaign workers.

The candidate should set down clear guidelines on dress and appearance for leafleters.

Each volunteer should be equipped with a few materials other than his leaflets, such as bumper stickers, order cards, or buttons, which can be given or sold to interested persons.

Every volunteer should be responsible for cleaning up litter in his area. People have an annoying tendency to throw leaflets away twenty or thirty feet from the person distributing them.

The first leaflet drive in a campaign may not go off very smoothly, with volunteers discouraged by lack of public response, or by the seeming futility of handing out leaflets. This is to be expected. No activity should be canceled just because it is not an immediate success. It takes time to iron out the defects in any operation and even more time for success to be apparent.

Voter Registration

Effective voter registration can provide the winning margin in any campaign. Registration of new voters may be done as a separate effort, or as part of other canvassing activities. One of the first things to determine about any district is how many unregistered voters there are and who they are. With that information and with knowledge of other registration drives being conducted in the area (by the party or by other groups), a candidate can decide whether it is worthwhile to conduct a major registration drive of his own. In any case, this decision should be made early, since registration deadlines often fall several weeks prior to election day.

Determining who the unregistered voters in a community are is easy in theory but painstakingly difficult in practice. The people most apt to be unregistered are the poor, students, young workers, and new residents. A quick estimate of the number of unregistered voters can be gained by comparing census figures with the number of registered voters.

The first step in conducting a registration drive is to locate unregistered persons by name and address. This can be done initially by comparing the police listing of residents with the voter registration list, although some persons will not appear on either list. A phone book with listings according to address rather than by name is also useful.

Once a list of unregistered persons is compiled, the process of getting them registered is mainly a matter of telling them how, when, and where to register, and possibly offering assistance to those who need rides or babysitters. The process of reaching them is similar to any other type of canvass.

Every campaign worker involved in registration should be thoroughly acquainted with registration procedures and legal requirements. For both the workers' and the public's benefit, a fact sheet on registration should be prepared by headquarters staff: exactly when and were voters in each area can register, what the registration deadline is, and other pertinent information, should be provided in full. This information helps registration canvassers deal with misinformation people sometimes have.

Voter Registration Interview

The canvass kit includes a list of all residents in the area you are canvassing, with the names of voters already registered checked off. It also includes a street map, leaflets, information request cards, buttons and bumper stickers, as well as fact sheets on voter registration.

Your basic job is to tell people how, where, and when to register, and to determine whether they are eligible to vote. Do not pressure people to register; just give them information. At the same time, you also wish to inform them about the candidate and encourage them to have a favorable attitude toward him.

Canvass only those voters who are not registered, but don't let them know this is what you are doing. You do not want to give people the impression they are being singled out or watched.

Try to engage each voter in a conversation, using the following dialogue. Use your own approach if you wish, but ask each of these questions in the same order given here.

1. Hello, _____name_____, my name is _____ and I am a volunteer for Bill Jones, who is running for school committee. As part of the campaign, we are conducting a voter registration drive. May I ask you a few questions?

2. Are you familiar with the Jones campaign? (Offer the voter a leaflet. If he is receptive, offer to send the voter more information.)

3. Are you registered to vote? (Note: You know very well that he is not, but that's all right.)

> A. If the voter answers No, offer him a fact sheet on registration and explain registration requirements and point out the registration deadline. If it seems appropriate, say that you can arrange for a ride to the registrar's office or provide a babysitter.

> B. If the voter answers Yes, thank him for his time and leave. Don't insist that he is wrong; after all, he may have registered even though his name is not on the list.

If at any time in the interview the voter seems resistant to your suggestions, thank him for his time and leave. There's no sense registering persons hostile to your candidate.

A registration canvass can be done by phone, by mail, or in person, or any combination of these. Direct personal contact is always most effective. Since a great deal of effort must be put into making contact with unregistered voters, a registration canvass should serve other purposes as well.

A canvasser who gives an unregistered voter the idea that he has been "tracked down" and is being pressured into registering, will make the voter a bit paranoid. It is best for a canvasser to lead up to the question of registration without indicating that the subject is known to be unregistered.

Considering the amount of effort registration of voters requires, campaign workers should not knowingly encourage the registration of voters who are probably going to vote for the opposition. This means two things: first, that registration drives should concentrate on neighborhoods that on the basis of voting patterns and other data seem likely to be heavily in favor of your candidate; and second, that canvassers engaged in registration should immediately back away from and forget about a person who seems to be leaning toward the opposition.

Headquarters Activities

The campaign headquarters is the center of all of the activities under discussion in this chapter. Not only is the headquarters staff responsible for scheduling and providing supplies for activities such as leafletting, canvassing, and registration, but it is also the place where a great deal of research and backup work for each activity is done. Headquarters also plays a role in the campaign just by being a noticeable presence in the community.

If headquarters is located in a conspicuous place and if people are encouraged to walk in off the street to ask questions, or just to have a cup of coffee, headquarters itself can be a motive force in the campaign and the community. If people walking by a storefront headquarters on a main street see an urn of coffee and a welcome sign in the window, they are likely to drop in and see what's happening. Those who do drop in should not be pressured to contribute to or take part in the campaign.

If headquarters is a place where people feel free to come just to socialize, it will quickly become more than just an office. Headquarters should be an accessible and pleasant place for people other than campaign workers to congregate. (Some limit must be placed on the social aspect of the office, however, or else no work will get done.)

The location of headquarters can by symbolic of the campaign's place in the community. If located in the heart of the candidate's base of support, headquarters may develop the aura of a sanctuary. If in a less friendly area, it can represent the campaign's front lines. Where to locate headquarters is thus a political question.

A. Lists

One major goal of headquarters staff should be to build a card file containing a full record of contact with every voter. Information ranging from party affiliation to attendance at campaign events can be slowly accumulated on individual file cards allotted to each voter.

The master file card (see illustration) is an amalgam of the records of all campaign work groups. Its final use, which will be discussed later, is to allow election day workers to know whom to bring to the polls. It is also a permanent record which can be used in subsequent campaigns.

Among the lists which campaign staff may gather, collate, and put to use are:

1. A list of all those who have contributed money or taken part in the campaign. This list is the most important resource a candidate has.

Master File Card

(kept for each voter)

Name

Address

Phone

Party Affiliation: Dem _____ Rep _____ Other _____ Ind _____

Registered: Yes _____ No _____   Support rating:
(See p. 121)

Contacts and Other Comments: 1.
    2.
    3.
    4.

Volunteer Card

Name _____ Phone _____

Street _____

Town _____ Ward _____ Precinct _____

AVAILABILITY: _____ Daytime _____ Evening _____ Weekdays

_____ Summer _____ Fall

Skills:

2. The list of registered voters. This essential campaign tool can be obtained from state or local officials.

3. A list of those who have voted in recent elections. This type of list is not available in every state, but can be an asset, particularly in a primary election.

4. List of residents. Some states, cities and towns keep lists of all residents according to street address. This list is likely to be inaccurate, but is still useful.

5. Party membership lists — available from party officials.

6. Organizational memberships lists — possibly obtained from officers or members of professional associations, civic groups, religious organizations, and so on.

7. A variety of lists may be obtained from candidates in past elections, or from other present candidates.

8. List of those who have contributed to candidates in past elections. These lists are on file with state or local election officials.

If campaign headquarters were on fire and there were time to save only an armload of material, the wisest choice by far would be the organization's lists.

B. Follow-up

Follow-up is another basic headquarters function. This includes answering campaign mail, sending thank-you cards after events and responding to requests for information or services a volunteer cannot provide.

C. Training Volunteers

Any time a new person volunteers, headquarters staff should assign him to a work group and see that he is trained. Staff must keep abreast of the problems of campaign workers and attempt to develop better methods for doing each job.

The Headcount

As election day nears, it becomes increasingly important to shift the campaign's emphasis to identifying voters who support the candidate and to converting uncommitted voters.

The headcount is the process of canvassing every registered voter, determining his preference, and assigning him a numbered rating. (In a primary race, the canvass would be limited to those eligible to vote in that election.) A one to four scale is commonly used, "one" indicating support for the candidate, "two" indicating a favorable attitude, "three" indicating indecisiveness, and "four" indicating apathy or support for the opposition. ("Fours" are people who should not be bothered again.) It is vital that this rating system be used uniformly. Every canvasser should be told the meaning of the numbers and a constant check should be made by supervisors to see that everyone is using them properly.

Planning for the headcount should begin four to six weeks before election day. The work of canvassers can include other functions such as registration, recruiting, and publicizing the candidate's positions.

By the time the headcount begins, the organization should have workers in every neighborhood and should have a good knowledge of the geography and political makeup of the community. This makes it possible to handpick canvassers for individual areas and to give each worker an assignment equal to his ability.

Headquarters staff should make up a kit for each canvasser. A kit should include a route map of the area to be covered and a list of voters to be contacted. It also should include material such as leaflets, bumper stickers, and information request cards. The list of voters to be contacted can be mounted on a "hard card," a piece of cardboard to which the list of voters' names and addresses is taped or pasted. (See illustration.)

Sample Hard Card

Main Street		Rating	Comments
1421	Cousins, James F.		
1421	Cousins, Elizabeth		
1421	Cousins, William J.		
1422	Fielding, Henry		
1422	Fielding, Mary		
1423	Coles, William		
1423	Anson, James		
1424	Black, Jane		

Rating: 1 — Definite Supporter
2 — Favorable Attitude
3 — Undecided
4 — Unfavorable

(This sheet should be mounted on a piece of cardboard, so that it is easy to work with and not likely to be lost or mutilated.)

The number of households listed on the hard card should be adjusted according to the population density of each canvasser's assigned area. Industrious canvassers may go through two or three hard cards a day, while others may take days to complete even one.

The names on the hard card should correspond to those on a set of 3″ x 5″ file cards, which should not be taken out of headquarters. After compiling information on his hard cards, a canvasser should return to headquarters and enter hard-card information onto the file cards.

Sample File Card

Phone: Rating:

     Name
     Address

Comments

When kits have been prepared, canvassers can be called together for meetings to receive training and instructions for the headcount. Special information on the characteristics of individual canvassing areas should be passed on to volunteers by other campaign staff with experience in those areas. For example, a canvasser who knows he is going into an opposition stronghold is much less likely to be discouraged by negative reactions than if he entered the areas with high hopes. A canvasser who gets a large number of negative reactions should be made to realize that whatever information he gathers is as important as that of a canvasser who works in a friendly area.

Ideally, each canvasser should be known to the people in the area he is to canvass. In some cases, a person can be too well known: someone known to be a perennial activist in all local causes might be more of a liability than an asset as a canvasser.

Every canvasser should be given a deadline for reaching the voters assigned to him. This deadline should be no more than two weeks after the time he is expected to begin working, since two weeks is enough time for a conscientious volunteer to complete a reasonable amount of work; also, the deadline must be early enough so that if the canvasser does not complete his work it can be done by someone else.

Four or five days after headcount kits are distributed, the headcount supervisor should telephone each canvasser to see whether he has any problems and whether his work is near completion. As the deadline approaches, more pressure should be applied to anyone who has not finished his work.

To guarantee that the headcount is completed, it is useful to recruit an elite group of canvassers who have shown zeal in their early work. These people can be used as trouble-shooters for completion of work in difficult or important areas.

Upon contacting a voter, a canvasser should try to engage him in conversation about the candidate, the campaign, and the issues. The conversation should never be permitted to become an argument: any canvasser who finds a hostile or defensive reaction from a voter should back away by saying something like "Well, thank you for your time. We just want to make sure everyone knows about Smith's candidacy." No conversation should last more than a few minutes.

The canvasser should always remember his two basic objectives: first, to disseminate favorable information about the candidate; second, to identify sympathetic voters and record their

Instructions to Canvassers

The canvass kit includes a "hard card" listing all registered voters in your canvassing area, plus a supply of buttons, bumper stickers, information request cards, and leaflets. You should wear a button and a name tag.

Canvass everyone on your list and return to headquarters when you are finished.

Vary the style in a way that is comfortable, but ask the voter the following questions in the sequence given. Do not put the voter on the defensive.

1. Hello, _____, my name is _____, and I am a volunteer for Bill Jones, who is running for school committee. I would like to speak to you and your (husband/wife) about Jones' position on issues in which you are interested.

2. What issues concern you most in this race?

3. Are you aware of Jones' position on those issues? (If the voter is not, give him a leaflet or offer to send him other literature.)

4. Are you familiar with Jones' campaign? Feel the voter out for a definite response. Don't get into an argument. If he is negative, thank him and leave. Be ready to offer more information.

Be as familiar with the issues and the candidate's views, but don't expect to be able to answer questions about the candidate's position. Have the voter fill out an information request card instead, and then see that headquarters answers the question or invite him to a coffee hour.

If the voter would like information about the opposition, suggest that he attend one of the opposition's campaign events.

If the voter seems receptive, offer him a button or bumper sticker. (If a sticker is accepted, offer to put it on his car yourself.) Also ask if he would be interested in taking part in the campaign. But don't be too pushy.

After you leave the house, fill out the hard card. Give most accurate rating you can:

1. definite supporter
2. favorable attitude
3. undecided or noncommittal
4. favorable to the opposition or unfavorable to Jones

sympathy on his data sheets so that they can be called and brought to the polls on election day.

Role-playing among campaign workers is a good means of training canvassers for dealing with the various types of reactions they will get from the public. It is also a good chance to point out the use of the one-to-four rating system.

In many cases, the headcount is a campaign's last or only contact with individual voters. The canvasser's interview should therefore be as positive an experience for the voter as possible. Any interest the voter displays should be promptly reinforced, for instance by sending him additional information or inviting him to a campaign event.

Rather than attempting to answer questions about the candidate's positions, a canvasser should offer to obtain the answer. (It is dangerous to let volunteers answer policy questions.) The canvasser should note the question on the hard card and have headquarters send out an answer. (People get so little attention from politicians that they are quite impressed when they are treated properly. Any invitation for further contact should be pursued.)

The headcount supervisor should keep in touch with canvassers at all times to see that the right procedures are being used in giving ratings and to see that follow-up on voter questions is done. Regarding ratings, any canvasser who turns in ratings consistently different from what other canvassers are getting should be taken off the job. That is, if one volunteer produces a group of rating cards in which 80 per cent of the voters are rated as "ones," while everyone else is getting about 40 per cent, then something is wrong. It may be that the canvasser doesn't understand the system, it may be that voters just like the canvasser, or it may be that the expression on his face when he asks questions indicates that he will be heartbroken if he receives an unfavorable answer. In any case, a canvasser getting unusual results should be assigned to some other job.

The headcount supervisor should also debrief canvassers as they complete their work, in order to identify problems in canvassing techniques or to learn about voter response to the candidate and his positions.

When the headcount is complete, the finished 3" x 5" rating cards provide the basic information for the final phase of the campaign: getting out the vote. Voters rated as "ones" or "twos" can be singled out as high priority targets for election day, while "threes" may be subjected to a final mailing or leaflet drive.

Many amateur canvassers mistake the difference between ratings. As a final precaution against bringing unfavorable voters to the polls, it is a good idea to double check the actual leanings of voters rated "two." This can be done by polling 50 to 100 "twos" in the last few days before the election. If the results are favorable, i.e., if at least 60 per cent of those polled are really "twos," all "twos" can be called out on election day. If less than 60 per cent are actually "twos," it is not worthwhile to bring them to the polls.

Getting Out the Vote

Depending on the expected size of the election day turnout, it may or may not be worthwhile for a campaign to conduct a major get-out-the-vote drive. It is especially important to have a get-out-the-vote drive in a primary election when the primary turnout is traditionally low.

Getting out the vote is a major undertaking. For a maximum effort, staff needed include poll-watchers, telephone canvassers, leafletters, neighborhood workers, drivers, and babysitters. Coordinating the activities of dozens of such workers requires detailed planning.

By the time election day arrives, everyone involved in the operation should know his job and be prepared to do it in the time available. Headcount rating cards must be processed, so that names and phone numbers of "ones" and "twos" are immediately available to telephone workers.

Election day workers have two basic tasks: to see that all "ones" and "twos" get to the polls, and to influence "threes" and "fours" who are encountered on the way to the polls. ("Threes" and "fours" should not be encouraged to vote.)

Election day activities generally begin the evening before — with last minute leaflet drives, rallies, block or house parties, or other means of reaching voters. The basic election day activities are as follows:

Hanging reminders on doorknobs. One means of getting a good turnout is to hang some kind of reminder tag on the doorknob of each sympathetic voter's home. This can be done in the early morning hours before people go to work, between midnight and dawn, though it might be unwise in some areas. Volunteers armed with maps and the addresses of "ones" and "twos" can work through the night hanging tags on doorknobs.

Leafleting. Outside polling places, factories, shopping centers, and other designated spots, volunteers may hand out sample ballots and leaflets.

Canvassing. Telephone and neighborhood canvassers can contact voters and shepherd them to the polls. When necessary, canvassers should be able to call upon babysitters and drivers. Drivers and babysitters should be recruited from the neighborhood they will serve.

Poll-watching. A poll-watcher has two distinct tasks — first, to make sure that fraud, machine breakdowns, or other problems do not interfere with the election; second, to determine who has voted, thus making it possible for canvassers to know who needs to be contacted.

Poll-watchers must be equipped with detailed instructions on what to do in emergencies such as when a machine breaks down at 6 p.m. and dozens of voters are denied the opportunity to vote. Local election officials and party representatives can be consulted for the planning of poll-watching arrangements. It is wise to arrange for a lawyer who knows election laws and is willing to be on call throughout election day.

The poll-watcher's real work in most cases consists of letting headquarters staff know which voters have already cast ballots. In most places, poll-watchers are permitted to stand near election officials and take the names of voters as they arrive at the polls.

The poll-watcher should be equipped with a list of registered voters on which the names of "threes" and "fours" are already crossed off. As "ones" and "twos" arrive at the poll, the poll-watcher crosses their names off. Then, at an agreed time, perhaps three or four hours before the polls close, the poll-watcher may take his list back to headquarters so that those whose names are not crossed off can be phoned. (There are several ways in which the activities of poll-watchers and canvassers can be coordinated. Where ample labor is available, the poll-watcher's lists can be checked by messengers every hour or two, for example, so that the poll-watcher stays at the poll until closing.)

Voter registration, the headcount, and the election day operation can provide the edge in any campaign. Many a candidate loses by a margin smaller than the number of people who would have voted for him if they had only arrived at the polls.

7

Opinion Polling

OPINION POLLING has become such a popular feature of American politics that candidates on even the local level have begun to practice the art. The word art is apt, since even the most sophisticated national pollsters are often wrong. In light of the frequent failings of the best polling operations, the local candidate who undertakes a poll of his own with amateur techniques should realize that he is taking a risk.

In spite of the risk, there are situations where it may be worthwhile for a local candidate to conduct his own poll. There are several types of data which even a relatively crude poll can determine with reasonable reliability. An amateur poll can determine:

1. Which of several issues is most important to the electorate

2. What voter attitude is on a given issue

3. How well known a candidate is in relation to his opponent or to other politicians

4. What are the strengths and weaknesses in a candidate's public image

5. Which issues are most strongly associated with a particular candidate

One drawback of opinion polls is that the type of information they are likely to yield is material that an astute observer of a small community should already know. This is especially true in the case of an amateur polling effort, which must limit itself to less sophisticated types of questions than a polling firm with computers, statisticians and sociologists.

Types of Questions

In any opinion poll, the simpler each question is and the simpler the composite set of questions is, the easier it is to conduct the entire polling effort. Since the interviewer, the voter, and the person analyzing poll results may each have a different view of the meaning of a question, deciding what questions to ask and how to ask them is a critical stage in the process of conducting a poll.

1. Minimizing variables. The fewer variables a question contains, the easier it is to ask, answer, and analyze. For example, the direct question "Do you intend to vote for Fred Salucci?" should yield a "yes," "no," or "I haven't made up my mind" answer.

This question offers the voter a clearcut, unmistakable choice, which requires no further explanation. The same is true of a question such as "Do you approve of the $200 pay raise the teachers just received?" (Yes, no, don't know.)

On the other hand, questions such as "How would you rate John Smith's performance on the school board?" (on a one to five scale) or "Which of the following issues is most important to you: —— ?" offer the voter too many possibilities to give answers which may not be clearly understood by analysts. Since the voters as a group may not answer the questions with uniform meanings, the results cannot be interpreted accurately.

In addition to the fact that complex questions or questions using numerical values may be misunderstood, such questions are also far more time-consuming to interpret.

2. Eliminating ambiguity. Misleading language can be a major source of difficulty.

The answer to the question "Which candidate do you like: Smith or Jones?" may not reveal much to the poll analyst. While Smith may come out the winner in the answer to this question, he may lose on election day for the simple reason that while the voters "liked" him, they did not consider him as qualified as Jones.

3. Supply as much information as possible. In order to give the voter maximum opportunity to reflect his real opinion, a question should offer as much information as it can without becoming unwieldy. For example, the question "Whom will you vote for: Smith or Jones?" might not yield as meaningful results as the question "If Smith were the Republican candidate and Jones were the Democratic candidate, which one would you vote for?" The second question gives the voter information he might not have known, but which would be important in determining his answer.

4. Giving the respondent a real choice. Any question which purports to offer the voter a choice should do so. For example, a voter who is asked "Which is more important to you: establishing a town recreation program or building a new town hall?" will give an answer. But his answer would not mean much if his real desire was to reduce property taxes.

There are also questions which theoretically offer a choice, but which say in essence, "Are you still beating your wife: yes or no?" For example, a voter asked whether he would rather pay for a new school or have students attend in double sessions might be embarrassed into favoring the former when he would actually favor the latter. A sound poll would ask the question differently. (And a wise politician would try to find a third course of action.)

5. Eliminating bias. In the complete questionnaire and in individual questions, it is vital to eliminate words or attitudes which will tip off the respondent to the "right" answer. This is much easier said than done.

It is absolutely essential that the respondent should not

know that the poll is being done on behalf of a candidate. This means a) that the interviewer must not tell the respondent the real reason for the poll; and b) that the nature of questions should not tell him.

A respondent who knows that a candidate is seeking his views is likely to tailor his answers to what he thinks the candidate wants to hear or what he knows the candidate does not want to hear. That is, he will try to "please" the candidate or to mislead the candidate (perhaps unconsciously) by giving different answers than those in which he believes.

To avoid tipping off the respondent, it is necessary to see that the questionnaire is not weighted toward questions about the candidate or toward questions that would immediately be associated with the candidate. If necessary, this weighting can be achieved by adding dummy questions to the questionnaire (i.e., questions the interpreter will not analyze at all). Since that is a poor use of the interviewer's and the respondent's time, it is better to ask questions about other candidates, or about other issues than those of most concern to the candidate. These questions can be arranged in a sequence that avoids any clustering of the questions most interesting to the interviewer, and avoids revealing to the respondent the interviewer's actual purposes.

Even where the purpose of the poll is successfully concealed, there still remains the problem of phrasing questions in ways that do not indicate what answer the *interviewer* wants to hear. Words commonly used to discuss any political issue quickly become loaded to a degree that their users may not even realize. The question "Do you support forced busing to achieve racial integration?" virtually supplies its own answer: No. So does the question "Are you opposed to giving black children the same educational opportunity as whites?"

The bias underlying the language in a question need not be so blatant to have an effect.

Whether it is the language or the content of a question

which supplies the respondent with an almost inevitable answer, any question that contains detectable bias is both a waste of an interviewer's time and a threat to the reliability of a poll. If the bias goes undetected by those conducting the poll, it is especially dangerous. If important judgments are made on the basis of the results of such a poll, the candidate will pay heavily for the poll's weaknesses.

6. Open-ended questions. Because of the difficulty any amateur is likely to have in combatting the problems mentioned above, open-ended questions are by far the most desirable in primitive polling operations. (By "open-ended," we mean a question which invites the respondent to give his full opinion in his own words.)

Since a polling operation in any small community need involve no more than 100 or so respondents, it is not a major task to sort out the answers to questions such as "What do you think was Mayor Smith's major accomplishment?" or "What is the city's most important problem, in *your* opinion?"

Including questions of this type in a poll makes work for the interviewer, since he must write down the respondents' answers as fully as possible. But it also makes for better insights into the way voters are thinking. The fewer numerical analyses involved in an amateur poll, the more reliable its results will be. The open-ended question is the least risky way to achieve a direct understanding of public opinion.

Choosing a Sample

The nature of the results obtained in a poll also depend in large part on who is polled and who is not. In order to assure that those who are polled represent a cross section of the people whose opinions are desired, it is mandatory that the people to be polled should be selected systematically. The decision on whom to poll should not be left with individual interviewers.

The sample chosen for a poll can be as broad or as narrow as the pollsters wish: a sample might consist solely of a) registered Democrats, b) all registered voters, c) only those who voted in the last election, d) registered voters in a certain age bracket, and so on. Whatever sample is chosen, the pollsters should know *whose* answers they are getting. A poll which obtained answers from, for example, every fifth person who passed by an interviewer on the street, might not mean very much. The results obtained in a poll of persons who are simply *residents* of a community would have different political significance from the results of a poll of registered Republicans.

Rather than simply picking 100 names out of a phone book or street directory at random, it is first necessary to decide what group a poll is intended to analyze. When that decision is made, the names of respondents to be contacted can then be chosen from the right category. (Once the category is chosen, the persons *within* the category should be chosen at random.)

No poll should be based on the answers of less than about 50 respondents, since a smaller sample is so narrow as to be misleading. With a voting district of up to 5000 voters, a sample of 50 or 100 persons is sufficient to obtain a reasonably reliable set of results. In a district of more than 5000 voters, 100 is the minimum size for a valid sample, while about 400 is the maximum useful size.

In a district with several radically different subgroups (e.g., poor whites, blacks, affluent whites), it is best to conduct a separate poll in each segment of the district, in order to guarantee that each subgroup's views are amply represented and that the differences between the opinions of the various groups can be determined.

Gathering Responses

Of the three basic means of interviewing respondents — by mail, by phone, and in person — it is best for amateur interviewers to use the telephone.

Mailed questionnaires or questionnaires handed out for return by mail are both undesirable because of the length of time they give for the respondent to frame his answers. Any respondent is tempted to try to give an answer which he thinks is the answer the questionnaire seeks, and second-guessing the questionnaire is easier for a respondent who is able to read all of the questions before answering. In addition, a mailed questionnaire is likely to be returned only by a small portion of those who receive it, and the people who return a questionnaire are liable to give quite different answers from those who do not return it.

The problem with having interviewers conduct polls in person is that amateur interviewers are too likely to reveal to the respondent what answer is desired to each question. Shifts in posture, changes in tone or voice level, and other personal mannerisms (usually unconscious) can easily give away an interviewer's personal opinion and thus influence the answer the respondent gives. While an experienced interviewer might obtain better results in person than on the phone, the reverse is the case with an amateur.

In addition to reducing any bias caused by the interviewer, the use of telephones for conducting a poll makes it possible for the interviewers to be supervised by the person in charge of the poll. A supervisor sitting in the same room with three or four telephone interviewers has the opportunity to judge and correct the techniques of the interviewers, and to monitor poll results as they come in. Whatever the other weaknesses of the poll, it can thus be assured that the interviewing was carried out properly.

Any interviewer who seems to be obtaining markedly different results from others should be taken off the job *immediately:* there is probably something in his manner which is causing respondents to answer differently.

An incidental advantage of telephone polling is that if there are two phones on the same line, a third person can listen in on the exchange between interviewer and respondent. Besides offering an opportunity to evaluate interviewers, this would permit the candidate himself to hear what the public has to say about him. This is a real advantage, since a poll is often a means of convincing a candidate that he must change his methods or his message to some extent. A candidate who listens in on thirty or forty conversations between a "neutral" interviewer and voters is likely to gain important insights into the public's perception of his candidacy.

Analyzing Poll Results

When the results of a poll are finally in and tabulated, that is the time for the candidate's poll-taking specialists to step aside and leave analysis of the results to the politicians. There are always several ways to read the results of a poll, and the final interpretation should be made not by a statistician or sociologist, but by those who best understand the political background behind the poll — including the candidate himself.

Especially in a case where a local "expert" has been given responsibility for running a poll, the people who conduct a poll are likely to consider it unchallengeable evidence for whatever conclusion they have reached on the basis of the results. In some cases, this may mean that the pollsters will insist that the candidate change his position on one issue, boost his identification with another, or alter his campaign style. While such opinions should certainly be taken into consideration, any change in campaign style and substance should result from the interpretation the candidate himself gives to the poll results.

A poll is likely to be wrong by a few percentage points on any given question. A candidate should always assume that a poll's results are at least slightly less favorable than they look.

8

Issues

THE LINES OF BATTLE in any campaign are drawn by the candidates. It is they who decide what issues will be discussed, whether the tone of the contest will be bitter or calm, and to what extent factors other than substantive issues will be paraded before the public.

There are many grounds other than issues on which elections are won and lost. In addition to personality, age or party, one could add professional background, political experience, geographic loyalty, social class, race, sex, religion, family background, wealth and education, to name just a few.

In a race where the candidates seem to be basically the same in their stands on the issues, each has the option of taking the similarity for granted — and then campaigning on some other basis — or of rejecting the apparent similarity and looking for ways to enlarge the differences that exist. The public will perceive the positions of two candidates as identical or similar only if both candidates wish that to happen.

When two candidates appear headed for a dramatic clash on the issues, each candidate likewise has the option to minimize the split. A candidate's decision to widen or narrow the gap between his positions and an opponent's should ultimately depend on whether it is to his advantage to do so. When the gap is particularly wide, however, it is usually the result of the fact that one candidate came into the race specifically to bring about a confrontation on grounds of principle or ideology. In that case, the other candidate may have great difficulty in minimizing the gap between them.

Types of Issues

In lining up a series of issues on which to base a campaign, it is helpful to distinguish between various types of issues. Very few issues interest everyone, and it is important to consider beforehand how many voters really care about a given issue and what is the extent of their concern.

The first type of issue for a candidate to identify is the "leverage issue," an issue which is the sole matter of concern to a given voter or group of voters. Just about anything can become a leverage issue if the circumstances are right. Abortion, school busing, and gun control are often leverage issues, but matters such as the construction of new apartments, zoning changes, or even the location of a new school can be leverage issues. Faced with a leverage issue on which he opposes a large segment of the electorate, a candidate is faced with the classic dilemma of the democratic politician: whether to stick to his guns and lose the election or whether to compromise his own stand on that issue in order to get elected.

Another useful distinction can be made between philosophical and mechanical issues. Issues such as civil liberties, sex education, or school integration revolve around questions of philosophy or morality. Other issues, such as poor garbage collection service, the need for a new public building, or inefficiency in a government agency, are argued not in terms of philosophy but in terms of dollars, convenience, or technical data. (There is naturally some overlap between philosophical and mechanical issues — as the question of whether a new highway is necessary — but the distinction can usually be made.)

On philosophical issues it is generally possible to take a clear and definite stand without fear that new information will later discredit that stand. But it is often unwise to make a heavy commitment to any one way of approaching mechanical issues; the cost of a new building, for example, could end up being twice what was expected. It is necessary to be a lot more flexible about mechanical issues than about philosophical issues.

There is also an important difference between general issues and particular issues: that is, some issues are of concern to the public as a whole, and others are of interest only to particular, often well organized, special interest groups. Everyone is interested in a tax increase, but only small groups of voters get really excited by matters such as prison reform, recycling waste, or nuclear reactor safety.

Developing detailed stands on particular issues is an effective means of gathering support from labor unions, trade associations, consumers groups, or other issue-oriented organizations. Issuing position papers on particular issues and seeking out speaking engagements before special interest groups are both effective means of winning the loyalty of such groups.

Identifying and dealing with general issues is a more difficult matter. Since relatively few politicians have a real instinct for what the public is thinking, it is unwise to place very heavy reliance on one issue or a single approach to an issue without carefully investigating public opinion. Above all, a candidate should be sure to go beyond his own circle of friends in trying to learn what is on the voters' minds. Political proposals should not usually be made public until those who will be most directly affected have been sounded out for their suggestions.

Picking Your Issues

There are always more issues available for discussion in a given campaign than either the candidates or the public are able to deal with effectively. Choosing what issues to work with is a matter of selectivity and emphasis, not a question of simply reacting to the dictates of either circumstance or the electorate. In deciding what issues to use in building a platform, a candidate should keep the following points in mind.

If an issue is important, beat the opposition to the punch on it. Study the issue, know it cold, and don't give the other candidate a chance to make it his issue.

Go after old issues in creative ways. Rather than merely criticizing a governmental agency for wasting money, for example, propose specific cost-saving devices or point out methods of measuring one agency's performance against its expenditures.

Seek out hidden issues that people talk about but which don't usually come up in elections. One fairly common example is the sheer frustration citizens often feel in trying to get civil servants or agencies to do their jobs (e.g., building inspectors, public utility commissions, or consumer protection agencies).

Be sure to discover the real reasons for public opposition to governmental policies or programs. The public often fails to understand the subtleties of political issues, but it is a candidate's job to provide that understanding.

Don't allow yourself to be bullied by special interest groups who demand that you take an extreme stand on an issue. Whether they are for you or against you, the most zealous exponents of a cause often have to be ignored. Organizations created for the promotion of a single political issue are unpredictable allies — at times your most dedicated supporters, but occasionally withdrawing their support with little provocation.

Instead of trying to speak to every available issue, attempt to give your campaign a theme out of which responses to individual issues emanate naturally.

Though it is necessary for a candidate to display an understanding of a variety of issues, it is equally necessary to develop a happy medium between being a single-issue candidate and having a shotgun approach. A candidate who tries to deal with too many points risks giving only a vague and confusing impression of what he stands for.

Political issues are often discussed in loaded language that makes it impossible to oppose the conventional wisdom. It isn't possible to prevent an opponent from using terms such as "handcuffing the police" or "busing little children," but it is possible to be sensitive to the nuances of meaning and to seek out new vocabulary or new levels of discussion when attempting to lead the public into an alternative approach.

Every politician must realize that he has only a limited amount of capital, and that to spend it all on one issue is usually foolhardy. A candidate can afford to oppose public opinion some of the time, but one who places no limit on doing so is pressing his luck.

Finally, assembling a group of issues into a platform is a process that usually requires a candidate to put his constituents' concerns ahead of his own. In order to represent a group of voters effectively, a candidate must be sympathetic to their needs, attitudes, and ideas. A candidate who has no feeling for the problems and even the prejudices of his district is not likely to be able to conceal the fact. Without a gut-level understanding of his constituents' thinking, a candidate will not be able to anticipate their reactions, see their objections to his ideas, or present his views to the voters with maximum tact and insight.

The Opposition

Choosing an approach to the opposition is as important a strategy decision as formulating policy on the most volatile issue. (Sometimes the opposition is the most volatile issue.) Whether he decides to ignore, attack, or merely disdain his opponent, a candidate should choose his course of action only after careful consideration of the consequences of each alternative.

It is dangerous to launch an attack against an incumbent without a firm understanding of his positions and his record as well as his standing with the public. A good starting point in deciding on strategy against an incumbent is to size up his strengths and weaknesses in terms of each of the following variables:

Voting record (Know an incumbent's voting record by heart.)

Positions on controversial issues

Service to constituents

Leadership role (Both in office and in other organizations.)

Priorities (What he has not done, as well as what he has done.)

Alliances (Both with individuals and with organizations.)

Party standing and loyalty

Personal factors: age, experience, character

Support (Who worked in or contributed to his last campaign?)

Patronage (Who benefits from his official actions?)

What to do with the information gained in each of these categories is a different matter than how to obtain it. It is important to realize that the same people who elected the incumbent are the ones who hopefully will elect you. In criticizing an incumbent, one sometimes comes dangerously close to criticizing the voters who elected him. Any criticism of an incumbent should be precise, careful, and well-documented.

Whether or not the opposition is an incumbent, another key point to consider is how visible the opposition is. If the opposition is relatively unknown, then any mention of him is likely to gain as much for him as for you. When two newcomers are in a race, they are in a name-recognition contest, and it makes little sense for one to make the other an issue.

A common occurrence in any campaign is for campaign workers to regard the opposition candidate as not merely the enemy but as evil personified. Within proper limits this kind of sentiment can be a source of motivation. When the negative feeling begins to generate ill feeling among members of the community, however, it is liable to boomerang. It is also a poor idea to build up antagonism against the opponent's supporters, since the more emotionally involved they become in his campaign, the harder they will work. Polarization is always a two-edged sword.

As far as possible, any candidate should emphasize his own positive qualities and ideas rather than attacking the opposition. A straightforward and good-natured campaign is much more likely to generate favorable reactions than one based on hatred or divisiveness. If and when a decision is made to criticize the opposition, the attack should be made in the least venomous manner possible, with the emphasis on the public welfare rather than on the personal feud between two persons seeking office.

What to Do When Attacked

The hardest thing to do in politics is to do nothing. As often as not, the best course of action to take when attacked is to say nothing and let the smoke clear so that a calm and rational assessment of the damage can be completed before a response is decided upon. In a moment of crisis, all campaign workers should be warned not to make any public statement without express approval by the candidate or campaign manager.

Whether a smear attack occurs months before the election or in the last few days, the victim's first impulse is generally to launch a counterattack immediately. The candidate and his supporters usually feel the sting of any criticism much more sharply than those outside the campaign, however. Since the public may be unimpressed by the charges made, it is always best to sit tight until it is learned to what extent a response is necessary. Quite often, an attempt to disprove an opponent's criticism only exacerbates the situation. Lastly, there is great risk in acting hastily in such a situation, since tempers are likely to have more influence than clear thinking.

Endorsements

As useful as endorsements can be, no candidate should delude himself by thinking that a series of impressive endorsements will roll him into office.

The assumption underlying the use of endorsements is that votes or allegiance can be transferred from one political entity to another. This is only marginally true. The endorsement of an influential politician or organization can reinforce the public's other contact with a candidate, but it can seldom do more than that. There are instances where an endorsement is decisive, but in those cases it is usually the absence of an endorsement that would have been noteworthy.

Primaries

Running in a primary and then in a general election often means running not just two campaigns, but two quite distinct campaigns.

Primary elections are usually decided by either party regulars or "true believers," the 10 to 15 per cent of the electorate who follow politics closely. The most important result of this fact is that a candidate often must deal with different issues in a primary than in a general election. Alternatively, he may be pressured into speaking much more forcefully on the same issues before the primary than he will want to do in the general election campaign.

Though many primary fights are just personality contests between candidates with the same views, it is also common for a pair of primary contenders to try to outbid each other as party loyalists or to push each other toward extreme positions on issues.

Although the majority of the electorate may not vote in a primary, they do read the newspapers. This puts the primary candidate in the difficult position of trying to win the support of partisans who will vote in the primary at the same time that he tries to keep his views in line with the larger, probably more moderate electorate he will face later.

9

Literature and Advertising

CAMPAIGN LITERATURE and paid advertising are the only means of communication with the voter over which a candidate has complete control. His other means of reaching the public — personal appearances, campaign workers, and news reports given by the press — are all subject to variables beyond direct control. Anything can go wrong when a candidate faces an unfamiliar crowd, a volunteer knocks on a door, or a reporter starts scribbling in his note-pad.

A leaflet, a letter, or an advertisement can be made to say precisely what it is intended to say to the voter — no more and no less. Whatever the drawbacks of political media, their great merit lies in this opportunity for controlled communication. Once a decision is made to use a leaflet, button, poster, or advertisement, its design and delivery to the voter should be executed with utmost care.

Even in a small community it is seldom possible for a candidate to reach every voter in person, or for campaign workers to spend much time with individual voters. As a result, literature and advertising must play an important role in even the most labor-intensive campaign. It is in any candidate's interest to have the best-designed literature and advertising he can afford.

It is not necessary to have a lavish media budget. One candidate can achieve as much with two or three thousand dollars well spent as another might achieve with $10,000. Media funds should not be spent wildly in the hope of achieving a shotgun effect. It is essential to have precise objectives for each outlay of funds for literature and advertising.

The design, delivery, and timing of literature and advertising should be coordinated with overall campaign strategy and planned in connection with particular phases of a campaign.

Every leaflet or advertisement a candidate uses should be tailored not only to his personality, issues, and style of campaigning, but also to the strategic and tactical objectives of his campaign. These objectives are different in every case: one candidate's election may depend on registering hundreds of new voters, another's on obtaining a large primary turnout, another's on simply making himself known to the public. Just as a candidate's other resources would be focused on such objectives, his literature and advertising should be too. There are dozens of types of campaign literature, from calling cards to position papers, but no candidate needs one of every type. Nor is a given candidate likely to need to use all of the advertising media, from newspapers to TV to billboards. While the various options should all be considered, some are bound to be a waste of money for a particular candidate, while others prove invaluable.

The Use of Literature

Campaign literature deserves high priority in the plans of a candidate running a small campaign. Literature can be produced cheaply, and various types of campaign literature can be used with far greater effectiveness and precision than advertisements. The purposes of campaign literature are as follows (advertising serves the same purposes):

1. To attract attention to the fact that an election is approaching. A great many voters need to be reminded that

election time is near, even when the election is only a few days away. This is particularly true of local elections. The mere existence of political literature is helpful because it sets people thinking about politics.

2. To organize campaign workers. Literature is an important tool in organizing a campaign. Not only does it attract the attention of potential workers, but it also gives them something to do. A candidate who has plenty of leaflets on hand can send workers out to distribute them.

3. To make the candidate known. This is the main purpose of all campaign literature. Sometimes it is a task just to get the public to recognize the candidate's name. In other cases more specialized needs such as calling attention to his record or his qualifications are involved.

4. To define campaign issues. While any leaflet produced by a candidate normally bears his name, some literature is best devoted solely to issues.

5. To cause voters to take specific action, such as:
  a. attending a campaign event,
  b. registering to vote,
  c. showing up at the polls,
  d. contributing funds or working in the campaign.

The following is a list of the more widely used types of campaign literature:

Leaflets, of every size, description and purpose.

Biographies of the candidate.

Calling cards, usually having a picture of the candidate, a thumbnail sketch of his views and a statement of his qualifications. These are generally used by the candidate in activities such as going door to door. They may be of any size but usually small enough to fit in a coat pocket without folding.

Position papers. Generally, these should not be more than 1000 words in length. Few voters are likely to read anything longer.

Campaign stationery and envelopes.

Campaign newsletters, which range in sophistication from mimeographed sheets to full-sized newspapers with glossy finish.

Endorsement letters (or leaflets), statements by individuals or groups endorsing the candidate and distributed in the same manner as other material.

Endorsement postcards. There are numerous possibilities in the use of postcards, but two variations are popular. In one, voters are handed preprinted postcards favoring the candidate, the cards being addressed to the candidate. If the voter sends the card in, he is listed as being committed and can be contacted on election day. In the second variation, called "Dear Friend" cards, anyone who is favorable to the candidate is asked to send to his friends a batch of postcards describing the candidate.

Reprints of favorable news articles. It is sometimes possible to have such reprints made up in large quantity on the original newspaper's press.

Invitations — to campaign events.

Volunteer name tags of paper, cloth, or any other material. These can be useful for volunteers working in difficult areas.

Sample ballots, especially where the ballot is complex.

Doorknob tags, small leaflets that can be hung on the doorknobs of committed voters on election eve to remind them to vote.

Public Service Literature. The easiest type of literature to distribute, and sometimes the most effective politically, is material that performs a public service. For example, a bus schedule bearing the candidate's name and picture is likely to get wide circulation in a city where public transportation is important. Other such possibilities include schedules of school athletic events, lists of government phone numbers (e.g., consumer protection services, welfare offices, pollution control bureaus), calendars of community events, or schedules of popular radio programs such as Spanish language programs in a Latin community.

Buttons. Buttons come in all sizes, shapes, and styles.

Bumper stickers. There are many types available, but the best are made of vinyl plastic; they are durable and easy to remove. Those made of paper tend to wash out upon getting wet and are impossible to remove neatly. Except in a brief campaign, the extra expense of vinyl is justified. Besides being highly visible and good for campaign morale, bumper stickers can be a source of revenue. (The same is true of buttons.)

Posters are inexpensive and can be quite popular if well designed. Silk-screening is the least expensive means of making posters and signs, and it is easy to learn.

Signs. Signs made to fit in windows, on lampposts, or on top of sticks (for lawns) are also cheap and can be effective.

Planning a Set of Literature

A candidate and his staff should determine early in the campaign what kind of literature is needed, when it is needed, and how it will be produced.

Early planning is essential in order to have all literature printed on schedule and to guarantee that the whole range of materials needed can be obtained at a price within the candidate's budget.

Planning a literature program involves several separate and far-reaching factors:

1. The first step in determining literature needs is to review the campaign's strategic problems and its schedule of events and activities. For example, if voter registration is a major campaign goal, leaflets must be obtained early enough for registration workers to use.

To make a reliable estimate of how much literature is

needed, it is best to work out a full scenario of the campaign and determine what kinds of literature are needed at each stage. A list of literature needs could be compiled in the following manner:

Election day:
> Sample ballots
> Instructions concerning the location of polling places and the hours they are open
> Doorknob tags
> Buttons
> Name tags
> General purpose leaflets

Pre-election rally:
> General purpose leaflets
> Issue leaflets
> Buttons
> Name tags
> Signs
> Posters announcing rally
> Leaflets announcing rally

Final canvass:
> Name tags
> Buttons
> Bumper stickers
> Canvassers' cards
> Leaflets

Coffee hours:
> Invitations
> Thank-you notes
> Leaflets
> Bumper stickers
> Buttons

Primary Election Day:
> Same types of material as on election day, but with obvious difference in content

Primary canvass:
 Same types of materials as final canvass
Registration canvass:
 Registration instructions
 Leaflets
 Canvass cards
 Bumper stickers
 Name tags

The more detailed a scenario, the more accurate an estimate of literature needs can be obtained. Accuracy in making an estimate makes it easier to decide how much can be spent on each category of material. (Plans for election day should be made early, so that the necessary materials can be purchased long in advance and so that there is no risk of running out of money for election day.)

2. In assigning priority to various materials, it is important to figure out how many voters will be contacted *only by means of literature* and will not be reached through campaign events or by intensive canvassing. For such voters, it is vital to see that the literature they receive is the best the campaign has to offer.

3. The third step in developing a literature program is to obtain bids, or to calculate the cost of each item needed. Whether literature is going to be sent out to printers or produced by campaign workers, there will be a wide range of unit prices available for each piece. This is the time to sit down with designers and/or printers to determine what is the best way to get the material you want at a price you can afford.

4. Before any decision can be made on what types of literature will be used, it is necessary to estimate how much manpower is available to prepare and deliver the final product.

The need for postage, envelopes, or computerized addressing processes can be eliminated if enough volunteers are available to address letters or deliver leaflets.

Delivery is often the most expensive aspect of a piece of literature. A campaign with a large corps of streetworkers can afford far more literature than one which must pay for postage every time it wants to reach the public.

5. With information on quantity, price options, and delivery, it is then possible to set a specific budget for each type of material needed.

6. The final phase in developing a literature program is designing the individual items needed. Ideally, a campaign's complete set of materials should be designed by the same person, or by a group working in close conjunction.

Aside from the need to obtain the greatest quality at the lowest cost, the most important aspect of designing a complete set of literature is that it should have a unifying theme. Each piece of literature (and advertising) should be designed so that it is linked both visually and conceptually to the other pieces in the set. This link (between leaflets, buttons, posters, stationery) can be achieved with various means — color scheme, typeface, slogan, photography, and logo. The object of this coordinated approach to design is to see that different phases of the campaign reinforce each other. Once the colors blue and white are associated with a candidate, for example, a voter is apt to develop a subliminal recognition of the candidate's literature.

Once a set of literature is designed, it should be thoroughly scrutinized, because when it comes back from the printer, it is financially and politically necessary to live with it.

Designing a Piece of Literature

No matter how inexpensive a piece of literature must be, excellence is both attainable and necessary. It is attainable because even a mimeographed leaflet can be attractively designed and correct in every detail. It is necessary because a candidate is as likely to be judged on the basis of his literature as on his competence in any other respect. If a leaflet is made up with ink that blurs or a typeface that is difficult to read, it may not be read at all, and the money and effort that goes into its production and delivery is wasted. If a letter is hastily written and mailed with mistakes in grammar and punctuation, those mistakes reflect directly on the candidate. There is no excuse for turning out shoddy campaign literature.

In preparing an individual piece of literature, there are four general questions to be considered:

1. What is the problem the piece seeks to deal with? That is, what action or response is it intended to bring about on the part of the recipient?

The desired response may be a specific act, such as registering to vote, or it may be a general response such as awareness of the candidate's qualifications and views on the issues. Every piece of literature has a goal which should be defined before the piece is designed. The design depends very much on the purpose of the piece. If registration is the goal, information about registration should be featured prominently. If recognition of the candidate's name and face are the goal, these should be highlighted.

2. What should the copy (text) be? If the purpose of a leaflet is to attract people to a rally, then a variety of information about the rally must be included.

A clear distinction should be made between what information *must* be included and what is optional. For example, it might be important to put the location of polling places on a leaflet circulated close to election day, but there would not be a need to do so on one distributed months in advance. There are also situations when it is best to omit certain information intentionally. A candidate wanting to emphasize his independence from his party might choose to omit the party name from his campaign literature.

3. What visual and emotional images should the piece project? Whether it is a bumper sticker or a position paper, a piece of campaign literature says more than the sum of its parts. The total visual impact of a piece of literature is as important as the accuracy of the facts it uses or the precision of the language it contains.

Pictures, graphic images, typeface, color scheme, and other factors convey important emotional messages — even when these messages are entirely unconscious or subliminal. A picture of a candidate sitting on a stoop talking to two children says something quite different from a head and shoulders shot. A leaflet using large print and plenty of white space has a different effect on *both* the eye *and* the mind from a filled-up page of fine print. It is a designer's job to seek out ways of conveying various effects, but the nature of the image conveyed is for the candidate and his staff to decide.

4. The final question — which affects design as much as it affects cost — is how will the piece be used? A leaflet which will be handed out by volunteers should be designed differently from one which is to be mailed. An envelope, for instance, should be designed to intrigue the voter enough to make him read the letter inside.

When these four general questions have been answered, the next step is to draw up a list of specifications for the designer. The illustration on the following page shows what kind of information a designer would need.

Two useful elements on any piece of literature are: a) a coupon which can be torn out and mailed to headquarters by those wanting to volunteer or contribute funds; or b) a business reply card or envelope for the same purpose. Every piece of literature should contain some indication of how to contact campaign headquarters.

The essential elements of the literature must be decided before a designer can begin his job. Included among those ele-

---

Outline for a leaflet on Urban Renewal

Use: Distribution in person by volunteers

Material: 8½″ x 11″ glossy paper, folded in half

Elements:
1. Photo of candidate
2. Photo of children in run-down neighborhood
3. Attached text
4. Tear-out coupon requesting volunteers and offering campaign literature, etc.
5. Logo: Democrat for City Council
6. Emblem of printers' union
7. Paid for by Committee to Elect Jones

Quantity: 10,000

---

ments is the copy, which should be concise and understandable.

Pitfalls to avoid:

Most amateur designers are afraid of leaving empty space on a page. Leaflets made up by amateurs are often filled with print, photographs, designs, and anything else that takes up space. White space on a page can be attractive and effective. There's nothing wrong with using wide margins and double-spaced type and leaving plenty of room around photos, illustrations, and headlines.

Amateurs often get verbose and don't know when to stop writing. Facts and rational argument are desirable, but it is possible to have too much of a good thing.

It is important to take community tastes into consideration in the design and the content of a leaflet. In one community there may be a prejudice against overly glib brochures, while in another it may be a mistake to rely heavily on detailed presentation of issues.

Simplicity of design is always a virtue. This applies to both content and graphics. There should be a single idea around which the content of a leaflet (or an advertisement) is organized and there should not be a hodgepodge of different styles of type, conflicting colors, or pictures competing for the reader's attention.

In dealing with printers, it is best to make a firm agreement on price and to put the specifications for design in writing. Without a written contract, anyone submitting an order is liable to be stuck with whatever errors a printer makes. It is also important to proofread the final product of a printer before it is formally accepted and sent out to the public.

In determining quantity, it is better to order too much than too little. Since a printer's major expense is in preparing for production (e.g., setting type), per unit costs drop sharply as the size of an order increases.

First and Last Literature Drives

There are two critical times for getting some kind of printed material out to the electorate: the beginning of the campaign, to attract notice; and the end of the campaign, to get out the vote.

Sending out literature early in the campaign serves two purposes: to direct public attention to the candidate and the campaign, and to begin recruiting workers and raising funds.

A final literature drive in the last few days of the campaign is important. If twenty or thirty names are on the ballot, each of those candidates will be clamoring for the public's attention in the last week of the campaign, and it is easy for a candidate to get lost in the crowd.

Newspaper Advertising

Newspaper advertising is a relatively effortless means of reaching large numbers of people. The two factors to consider are how much it costs for an advertisement and how many people the ad will reach. Graphic design, size, and location are the three determinants of both the cost of an ad and its probable impact.

Newspaper advertising suffers from two weaknesses not shared by direct mail, leaflets, or other printed material. First, it is inflexible. An advertisement appears only once. A letter or leaflet can be delivered, distributed at a rally or a coffee hour, or left on tables in public places. Surplus copies can be stored for use at a later date.

A leaflet or letter is more durable than an ad; few people cut ads out of their newspapers, while a leaflet may sit on someone's desk or car seat for days before being read.

In addition to being inflexible in use, advertisements reach an audience which cannot be defined clearly. Though a newspaper may claim readership in 20,000 homes, that does not mean 20,000 people read every ad. A leaflet delivered to 20,000 homes is bound to be seen by someone in every home. Also, no paper will reveal which 20,000 or 30,000 homes it reaches; in that sense, advertising is to some extent a shot in the dark. A leaflet or letter can be sent to precisely the homes the candidate wants to reach. In terms of flexibility and precision, literature is a sounder buy than an advertisement.

There are three good reasons for buying newspaper advertisements: convenience, credibility, and visibility. Since newspapers are the most important source of information about local politics in any community, newspapers are a good medium for political advertisement.

Concerning credibility, it is sometimes necessary to use newspaper ads to show that a campaign is serious. Just as some voters judge a campaign's credibility by the quality of its leaflets, others will not take a candidate seriously until they have seen his face in an advertisement.

A candidate with low visibility may be forced to purchase ads in order to break into the public consciousness. Especially when the opposition is well known or is running frequent ads, this can be a reason for spending money on advertisements.

Advertisements are also good for getting publicity quickly when it is necessary to make an announcement or respond to some issue. An ad can be placed in a paper in a fraction of the time it takes to prepare and deliver a leaflet.

Almost all of what was said earlier about literature — in regard to purpose, unity in design, timing, content, and preparation — also applies to newspaper advertising. There are several other factors any potential advertiser should keep in mind:

1. Especially in the political season, it is often necessary to reserve or pay for advertising space well in advance. With a small paper it may be necessary to request space several weeks ahead of the time an ad will appear.

2. A candidate planning a long series of ads may be able to get a special rate.

3. In designing an ad, it is important to pay close attention to the format of the paper in which it will appear. A designer should be familiar with the typeface, headline sizes, photographic limitations, and other aspects of the paper. In some cases it makes most sense to use the typeface the paper normally uses, but it can also be effective to use a totally different style.

4. As in many campaign activities, when the planning or execution of a particular project is too sophisticated or complicated for the staff to handle, the services of a professional should be considered. If a heavy advertising budget is expected for more than a few newspapers, an advertising specialist's fee and advice can save untold time, money, and anxiety.

5. Another useful option in advertising is to have a supple-

ment made up and inserted into the paper. Extra copies can be obtained for distribution later in the campaign. For example, it would be possible to have a four-page section included in the daily run of a paper and have the publisher produce an extra 10,000 units of the insert.

6. Rather than using ordinary advertising techniques, it is possible to buy space in which a column written by the candidate can be printed on a regular basis.

7. In addition to regular newspapers, it is a good idea to investigate the possibility of advertising in other local organs such as shoppers' guides, club publications, athletic programs, etc.

8. Proofreading is absolutely essential. It is best to place an ad well before the deadline and then ask to see the final product before the paper goes to press. While editors will normally reprint an ad free of charge if printers make a mistake, that is sometimes small consolation. Small weeklies are particularly likely to make serious mistakes in printing.

TV and Radio Advertising

Unlike either literature or printed advertising, radio and TV ads provide limited opportunity for most local candidates. This is so because radio and television advertising time is usually so expensive, and because radio and TV ads have to be much more carefully produced in order to get listener attention.

Any factual or theoretical material included in an electronic ad must be unmistakably clear the first time around. Unlike a reader with a leaflet in his hand, a radio listener or TV viewer cannot play back a sentence he did not hear properly or did not entirely understand.

Television advertising is not a realistic option for 99 out of

100 political candidates. It is almost always formidably expensive and can be a complete waste of money if it is not done with skill. The only candidates for local office who might be interested in TV advertising are those in thinly populated rural areas served by a TV station serving an audience that coincides roughly with the political district, or in areas served by cable television networks or UHF stations that have far lower advertising rates than the usual television station. Even a candidate in a district with 100,000 voters is probably squandering his money if he purchases time on a station serving 500,000 or one million viewers, as is usually the case in urban and suburban areas.

Radio advertising, however, is within the reach of a great many candidates, particularly those in small cities with local stations. While radio advertising is also a sophisticated medium, it does not present as many production problems as television.

The creation of a radio or TV ad is a difficult matter for the amateur because of the technical skill and equipment required. Production of a radio or TV ad can be expensive in itself, quite apart from the cost of air time.

It makes little sense for a candidate operating on a low budget to hire an advertising agency. Paying for the services of an agency is worthwhile only if the agency will be given enough business to make a substantial profit. An agency will not devote its best people to small accounts.

The best course for a candidate who produces only one radio or TV ad (to be used over and over) is to find an expert willing to volunteer his services, or else to draw on the staff of the station. Most stations are cooperative in making their equipment and staff available to help produce an ad.

Any station manager will be glad to discuss whatever studies are available on the station's listening audience, and on the audiences of individual programs. Ad time should be purchased only for specific target audiences, and should be run at a time of the advertiser's choosing.

Free Time and Paid Time

The more unpaid advertising (news coverage) one receives, the less paid advertising of any kind is necessary. A candidate who works aggressively to keep his name in the news (by actually doing things that make news) won't need as much paid advertising. A candidate should judge his public relations advisers not just by how well they design advertisements but also by how well they succeed in getting free news coverage.

10

The Press

A LOT OF POLITICIANS go wrong in their dealings with the press because they fail to keep one basic fact in mind: the press is the one source of public information that a politician cannot control and should not be able to control.

The job of reporters and editors is to strip away the public relations veneer from a politician's words and actions and to give an independent account of his doings. No candidate is likely to get the kind or amount of press coverage he thinks he deserves unless he has an editor in his pocket. The best a candidate should hope for is to get a fair shake from the media. How to do that is the subject of this chapter.

For most local candidates, dealing with the media is not a terribly complicated task, although it does require close attention. The media serving the typical small community usually consist of a few weeklies, a local or area-wide daily, one or two radio stations, and possibly a television station. A candidate's goal is to get the attention of each of these outlets as often as possible, and once he has their attention, to do what he can to guarantee that the coverage he gets is favorable.

A candidate should visit each editor and station manager at the beginning of his campaign. A sensible time to do this is just prior to making an announcement. Editors are used to having politicians come in to pay their respects. This visit is an opportunity for a candidate to explain his candidacy, sound out an editor or manager's political leanings, and learn what the paper or station's ground rules for political coverage are.

A lot of reporters and editors, regrettably, take the view that local candidates are not particularly newsworthy. A major reason for this is undoubtedly that it takes a lot of time and news space to cover local politics properly, and editors are often far more concerned with their budgets and their profits than with giving good news coverage. Some papers are content simply to run brief announcements of local candidacies and print nothing more until within a few days before an election. Many a candidate finds that the only time his campaign receives coverage is when something embarrassing happens to him or his opponent, or when the two clash on an especially controversial issue. Radio and television stations, often hiding behind the FCC's "equal time" policies, are even stingier than newspapers in covering local campaigns.

The visit to an editor's office is the time to ask what a paper's policies on political reporting are. A candidate should ask what types of information are printed as news, how releases should be submitted, and when deadlines are.

Regardless of what a paper or station's expressed policies are, a maximum effort should be made to attract regular coverage. Every news story, announcement, or editorial that mentions a candidate is free publicity. News coverage is likely to have more impact than paid advertisements.

In dealing with the press, there are several other points that any candidate should keep in mind:

1. In order to be written about, it is necessary to be newsworthy. A candidate who is ignored by the press should take a second look at his public relations techniques and at his own words and actions before coming to the conclusion that reporters are conspiring to keep him out of the news.

A candidate who speaks in cliches or generalities will not

distinguish himself from the dozens of other local politicians the media are also covering.

2. Establishing personal rapport with a number of reporters is always useful for a candidate. Even if his relationships with the press don't blossom into friendships, a candidate who knows the individual interests, specialities, and idiosyncrasies of various reporters is likely to be able to attract coverage more often than one who doesn't.

3. Being available when a reporter calls is a necessity for any candidate who wants extensive coverage. Every candidate should see to it that a reporter who wants to contact him knows where to find him night or day, or at least knows how to find him. In addition to giving reporters his phone numbers, a candidate should make sure that campaign staff knows where to find him when a reporter calls. Since any reporter normally works on a tight deadline, he often cannot wait two or three hours for a return call.

A candidate who makes himself unavailable to the press will find that they will stop trying to contact him. In some situations, a candidate will suffer by being unavailable, such as when he picks up the morning paper to read a damaging story about himself which includes the statement that "Jones could not be reached for comment last night."

4. The best way to gain a reporter's respect and gratitude (and thus to get favorable coverage) is to play it straight with him. Any question, no matter how awkward, should get a direct answer. Any good reporter knows when he is being dodged or gulled by a politician, which is why so many reporters get cynical about politics and develop hostility toward politicians. A politician who gives direct answers to direct questions will quickly gain the appreciation of reporters in general.

This doesn't mean that a politician has to cut his own throat when faced with a question he isn't prepared to deal with immediately. There are a lot of situations where it is possible to buy time in order to check on facts or consult sources. The questions a politician evades with noncommittal responses will cost him valuable credibility. A "no comment" should be any politician's last resort.

5. Doing as much of a reporter's work for him as possible is another means of increasing the amount of coverage a candidate gets. Press releases, texts of speeches, and other pre-printed materials do much to make a reporter's lot easier. In reducing the amount of note-taking a reporter must do, a candidate not only wins a little gratitude but decreases the probability of being misquoted.

Reporters thrive on facts, figures, and quotable quotes. More so than with perhaps any other campaign audience, a candidate dealing with the press should be armed with solid facts and should not hesitate to display them. A brief remark can easily sum up a position on any issue, but it takes more than a one-line quote for a reporter to write a news story.

A candidate should not be afraid to be a bit long-winded in presenting the details of his case to a reporter. At the same time, he should cultivate the art of summing up his thoughts in crisp phrases which make good quotes.

6. It seldom pays to get angry with the press. When dealing with reporters, self-discipline should be a politician's cardinal virtue. No politician should let himself blow off steam at a reporter without careful consideration of the effect his statements will have on both the reporter and the public.

Any candidate who loses his temper in front of reporters is doing so in front of the whole electorate. Anything he says is liable to fly back in his face off the next day's newspaper pages. In man to man fights with reporters, politicians always lose.

Politicians need reporters more than reporters need politicians. A politician who has a spat with a reporter, especially in a small community, is likely to be cutting his own throat, since he will need to talk to the same reporter again. It does no harm to point out a reporter's mistakes, however.

There are times when a candidate has reason to be angry with the coverage he gets, particularly when the editorial policy of a paper is directed against him. When this is the case, the best course of action is to confront the editors of the paper in person. There are a lot of times when a frank talk with an editor can settle what seemed to be a permanent state of enmity.

Even when there is no chance of getting fair coverage from a given editor or publisher, a candidate should weigh his options carefully before taking on the media.

What Is News?

What is considered news by one editor may be considered nonsense by another. The news standards of editors vary not only in what they are willing to print or put on the air, but also in how much trouble they are willing to take to get a story. Where one editor might be willing to print advance announcements of all of a candidate's campaign events, another will toss his every press release into a wastebasket. Where one will assign a reporter to cover a campaign on a regular basis, another will have occasional short stories written by whoever is available.

Depending on an individual editor's standards, news coverage is likely to come in any of the following categories:

1. Announcements. Beginning with his candidacy, any candidate has various announcements he wants to make public. Topics of such announcements include the formation of campaign committees, the opening of headquarters or other offices, the beginning of a signature drive, or commitments of support from influential groups or elected officials.

2. Public appearances. Any time a candidate is scheduled

to appear at a significant event, advance notice of the time and place of the appearance may be the subject of a news release. (A significant event can be anything from a coffee hour to a $50-a-plate dinner, depending on the news outlet in question.)

Press releases heralding a candidate's appearance somewhere should indicate why it will be of interest to both the public and the press. For example, if a candidate plans to make a major speech on some campaign issue, it is essential to give reporters advance notice of his intentions and some indication of the speech's content.

3. Action by a candidate. Any time a candidate *does* something other than what candidates usually do, his actions should be called to the attention of the press — if possible, in time for reporters to watch him do it.

Having the candidate actually *do* things during the campaign is the best way of making him newsworthy. The type of actions referred to here range from bringing a class action suit against a government agency to showing concern about ecology by canoeing the length of a polluted river. The rule in planning such activities is that they should be related to the office the candidate is seeking. For example, it would not be particularly pertinent for a school committee candidate to take up the banner of a citizens' group fighting pollution in a local pond.

4. A candidate's position on issues. News releases or position papers can be the raw material for news stories. Because most printed material submitted to the media without being linked to an event is liable to be regarded as mere propaganda, any document intended to be the subject of a news story should be exceptionally well prepared. A good example of this type of document might be a mayoral candidate's detailed plans for the reorganization of city government, a subject that might not lend itself to a speech or debate. (A small weekly might be happy to print such a document in full.)

In somewhat the same category are news releases on day to day developments in the campaign — on actions by the opposition or on other situations inviting the candidate's comment.

5. Editorials and columns. Without friends at the paper, a candidate is not likely to have much influence on what columnists or editorial writers say about him. What he can do is to make sure that they are fully informed of his views and receive accurate information. This can be achieved by seeing that such writers personally receive copies of all campaign literature. (In the case of any large paper, for example, two copies of each press release might be submitted — one to the news desk, another to the editorial writer.)

Writing a Press Release

There is nothing difficult about writing a press release. It's just a matter of observing a few simple conventions and writing in newspaper style. The key point to remember is to present information in a press release in order of importance, so that the main idea is contained in the first paragraph, and each succeeding paragraph contains less important information than the one before it. (This is the way newspaper articles are usually written, so that an editor short of space can cut the length of a story by eliminating the last few paragraphs.)

Since editors of many small papers print press releases verbatim, it is best to use simple language and short sentences, again in newspaper style.

Other common features of press releases are: a headline, indicating the gist of the release's content; a release date, the date and hour when the information may be made public; the name of a contact, a person who can be called by a reporter who wants more information; and the use of the word "more" at the bottom of each page but the last, with the number "30" used to indicate the end of the release. (See sample release.)

Normally it is best to limit a press release to about 500

Sample Press Release

JONES PROPOSES NEW RECREATION AREA

Release date: 10 a.m.,
January 14, 1973

For more information,
contact Leo Hurley
971-1600

Middleton — Purchase of the 1600 acre Groton Estate as a recreation area for city residents was recommended last night by Stanley Jones, a candidate for the Middleton City Council.

Speaking at a meeting of the Middleton Civic Association, Jones pointed to the almost complete lack of public recreational facilities in the Middleton area and said that the Groton Estate would meet a growing need. He estimated the cost of the estate at $500,000.

"Public purchase of the Groton Estate before it is taken over by private developers is Middleton's last chance to give the city's residents a convenient and fitting recreation area," Jones stated.

"The population growth in this area and the development of almost all the area's woodlands for housing and industry have made the need for publicly owned land a critical problem here. If the city does not act before it is too late, Middleton will never have a decent public recreation area," Jones added.

Describing the historic estate's numerous natural resources, Jones said it could be made to serve numerous community needs. He said plans he has outlined for the estate include provision for boating, skiing, athletic grounds, and a picnic area, as well as for conservation areas. He noted that Paradise Pond, a 75 acre pond, is one of the few unspoiled ponds in the Middleton area. Jones presented a detailed plan for development of the private estate which he said he had drawn up with the assistance of a committee of local citizens.

"Purchase of the estate will be a major investment for the city, but it will be an investment well made," Jones stated. "The question is not whether we can afford to buy the Groton Estate, but whether we can afford to let this beautiful natural resource be lost forever to the community," he stated.

words, on the assumption that any reporter who wants more information will take the trouble to phone.

Whenever a long statement such as a speech or position paper is made public, it should be accompanied by a press release giving a summary of the statement and explaining the background behind it.

The important point about a release date is that it is an attempt to guarantee that one reporter or one media is not given an advantage over another. For example, if an important local newspaper reaches the street at 2 p.m., and a release is sent out at night, attaching a release date of 2 p.m. the next day assures that people will not hear the information in the release on the radio before the newspaper is published.

It is important not to use release dates in obviously discriminatory ways. For example, if the local weekly publishes on Wednesday and a candidate wants to guarantee that the weekly is not "scooped" by a daily, he may be tempted to make Wednesday the release date for many of his press releases. If a competing daily newspaper's editor receives a release on Monday and the release date is Wednesday, it will be quite clear to him what the candidate is doing, and he will resent having to hold the release for two days. (There is a good chance that if the news is important he will not be willing to wait that long, which means that the release date will mean nothing.)

This last point brings up the subject of favoritism toward one or another media outlet, a tendency that is seldom likely to bring as much advantage to a candidate as he might be led to believe. A candidate should give preferential treatment to a reporter or editor only when it is unmistakably to his advantage to do so. If one outlet gives him consistently generous or favorable coverage, it might be worth his while for a candidate to reciprocate with preferential treatment. When that is not the case, he should be as evenhanded as possible in dealing with various media. If two reporters are in competition, a candidate should think twice before giving one an advantage. What he gains in gratitude from one he is liable to lose in terms of resentment from the other.

Releases for TV and Radio

Any release that is sent to a newspaper can also be sent to a television or radio station. Because of the technical difference in the needs of electronic media, however, it is sometimes easier to get radio or TV coverage by catering to their special needs. Since the electronic media are particularly concerned with airing news that is "up to the minute," it is important to see that radio and television stations receive releases as quickly as possible. Depending on the arrangements recommended by the station manager, it is often a good idea to telephone news releases to radio and television stations instead of sending them in by mail. (A candidate should not hesitate to telephone a release to a newspaper either.)

In addition to informing radio station personnel of his appearances, positions, and other announcements, it is possible to meet the special needs of radio in two ways. If a station is unable to send anyone to cover the event a candidate wants reported, he might arrange to visit the radio station before or after the event in order to have his comments taped or aired. Alternatively, the candidate himself, using a tape recorder, can dictate his statement onto a tape and have it brought to the station along with a printed release. If the station uses his message, the dollar or two it costs for a tape cassette is well spent. (This should only be done after checking with station personnel on the technical details, such as what type of tape they want used.) In the case of a speech to be delivered at a dinner, for example, a candidate could tape some or all of his prepared speech and have it in the station's hands by the time it is delivered at the dinner.

It is more difficult to attract television coverage than to get radio or newspaper coverage. This means that a candidate must be more thorough and more imaginative in planning ways of attracting television coverage. Since it is expensive for a station to send out a film crew, it is necessary to virtually guarantee a station that its efforts are worthwhile.

Photographs

Most dailies and some weeklies have their own photographers. With such papers, a candidate needs only to provide the paper with one or more head-and-shoulders shots for the paper's files. Similarly, a television station can be supplied with color slides.

Smaller papers are likely to rely completely on a candidate for the pictures they use. In these cases it is useful for a candidate to have his own photographer and to send in pictures with press releases. It is important to determine beforehand what technical requirements photos must meet in order to be published.

A Final Word

Just as a candidate cannot hope to control what the press will write about him, he will seldom be able to guess when the press will show interest in him. An editor's opinion of what is important is seldom the same as a politician's. No candidate should be surprised to find what he considers a major press release ignored, nor should he be surprised to have reporters start phoning him when he least expects it.

The objectives of a campaign's press efforts are to attract publicity, to present the candidate's perspective, and to see that the press has access to complete and accurate information. It is a press secretary's job to keep a steady flow of information going to the media and to try to see that the record is kept straight. If that job is well done, the amount and type of press coverage the candidate gets depends on luck and on the competence and integrity of the newsmen he is dealing with.

11

Six Candidates

No CAMPAIGN CAN BE RUN according to a script. The experiences of the six candidates whose campaigns are discussed here show that there are numerous ways of becoming a candidate and of winning an election.

Each of the candidates we interviewed for this chapter ignored one or more of the campaign tools recommended in this book. In some cases this was the result of a conscious decision. In other cases it was the result of lack of manpower or time. None of them ran an ideal campaign in the sense that every available tool was used, but every one of them won. In addition to having won, the six have several other characteristics in common. Each was a progressive candidate seeking office for the first time, waged a grassroots campaign mobilizing wide community support, and had a modest budget.

Houston, Texas:
State Representative Ron Waters

Being at the right place at the right time is the quickest way to prominence in any career, and nowhere is that more true than in politics. An appealing and competent candidate with a good organization has a fair chance of winning any election, but there are few politicians who attain office without a share of luck. In many cases, luck means the difference between having a chance to run and win and never having a decent chance at all.

In the case of Ron Waters, luck took the form of a state Supreme Court decision which put an end to the use of large, multi-member legislative districts. These districts had made the legislature a bastion of entrenched party polls having the wealth and power necessary to wage expensive campaigns over wide geographic areas.

In the fall of 1971, prior to the court decision, Waters was a twenty-two-year-old University of Houston senior with several years of political experience to his credit but with little chance of reaching office in the near future.

"I've wanted to run for some kind of office since I was eighteen. I was doing all of the things that you were supposed to do to work yourself up the ladder as a candidate," Waters states.

Indeed he was. He was president of the Young Democrats at the University, a member of the executive committee of the county Democratic Party, a veteran of campaigns for Ralph Yarborough and other liberals, and regional coordinator of Countdown '72, a nationwide youth registration effort. In addition, he was active in several community and statewide organizations.

In spite of these credentials, Waters had neither the money nor the recognition necessary to mount a campaign for municipal office in a city the size of Houston or for a legislative seat in a multi-member district.

"Under the old multi-member districts it would have taken me two to eight years to work my way into the position I'm in now where it is financially feasible for me to run a campaign," Waters stated during his campaign.

In October, 1971, however, a court ruling resulted in the creation of single-member legislative districts, and Waters immediately saw the significance of the ruling. The smaller districts suddenly made it possible for a candidate such as he to win without spending exorbitant amounts of money.

When the boundary lines of the new districts were announced, prospective candidates were thrown into a frenzy of speculation over their chances of winning in various districts. A two or three week game of political hopscotch ensued. Waters was living in what turned out to be a conservative district and was looking around for one where his prospects would be brighter. "At one point I had two or three apartments," he said of his search for a political base.

Casting his eyes across the district boundary into the nearby 79th district, Waters spotted his opportunity: "I couldn't believe they had put all those liberal Montrose precincts together. My first impression was 'Hell, a radical's going to get elected there.'" (Montrose is Houston's version of Greenwich Village.)

Asking around to find out who else might be running in the district, Waters learned of five or six prospective candidates. One of these was thirty-four-year-old Ann Lower, a writer and local party activist who would later become Waters' campaign manager. Ms. Lower urged Waters to run, saying she would bow out if he moved into the district.

Continuing his survey, Waters contacted the Democratic precinct judges (precinct leaders) in all twenty-one precincts of the district. "Out of twenty-one precinct judges, there were eleven who were liberal, and I got commitments from nine of them," Waters recalls. With that much support, he found an apartment in the district and went to work.

"I didn't know how I was going to raise the money," he said of his decision to run, but he did know that if he waited two more years it was likely that someone else would gain a grip on the district and Waters would be shut out.

The 79th legislative district, in which Waters and five other Democrats were to vie for their party's nomination in May, is roughly ten miles long and two miles wide, embracing a 70,000 person segment of Houston's population of 1.2 million. While it does contain the several liberal Montrose precincts that attracted Waters to it (including large contingents of freaks and homosexuals), the remainder of the district is a mixed bag. Of the twenty-one precincts, four are solidly black, one is Chicano, two consist of wealthy, conservative whites, and seven or eight more of older low-income Wallacite whites. "The majority of the district is poor, overwhelmingly poor," says Waters.

As he soon realized, various factions in the district were bitterly hostile to one another: the whites hated the blacks, the blacks hated the Chicanos, and the freaks just wanted to be left alone. Solidly Democratic (with only 2000 Republicans among 26,000 registered voters), the district was still not likely to go to a liberal without a fight. A conservative Democrat who played his cards right could easily send the liberal camp into confusion by playing off one out-group against another.

That, apparently, was just what Waters' chief opponent had in mind. He was a former state representative who, after being defeated in 1970, had gone to work as an aide to two other legislators. He had helped draw the boundary lines for the new district, and had earmarked it for himself.

The remarkable aspect of Waters' victory is how wide a spectrum of support he was able to bring together in this diverse district, and how he did so while adhering to what must have been one of the most liberal platforms in the state of Texas. While taking outspoken stands in favor of gay liberation and the legalization of abortion and marijuana, Waters was also able to attract the support of the Houston firefighters' and teachers' unions and the local chapter of the Steelworkers of America.

Very early in the campaign Waters realized that the only way to win was to find the common denominator of the several mutually alienated groups in the district. "The only thing the people in this district had in common was economics," he found.

Accordingly, Waters' speeches, his campaign literature, and the activity of his canvassers all focused on a series of economic issues bound to strike a chord in any voter's mind:

1. Waters favored the use of a corporate income tax to replace the state sales tax. The only other candidate who made any real headway had supported the sales tax during his previous time in the legislature.

2. With property taxes a thorn in every voter's side, Waters advocated equalization of the tax rates for residential and commercial property. He also proposed tax rebates for elderly homeowners, a measure the former legislator had voted against.

3. Long before his campaign, Waters had organized a Nader-style group to work for reform of the state's auto insurance rate-setting system. Carrying the issue into the campaign, he found that even the most conservative elements in the district were willing to ignore his youth and relative radicalism when he began talking about insurance. "Per person, per house," he discovered, "they picked that as the most important issue."

4. Waters also aroused community interest, especially among blacks, in his proposals for state action in the construction of low-cost housing, medical facilities, and recreation areas.

With his economic issues and with frequent emphasis on the need to reform the corruption-ridden Texas legislature of which his leading opponent had been part, Waters found a wide base that was relatively unworried by his stands on marijuana, abortion, gay liberation, women's rights, and police brutality. He won the support of unions with a strong prolabor stance and the endorsement of the Houston teachers' union with his views on education. He forged a coalition out of as unlikely an assembly of backers as could be found in American politics.

The campaign was stretched out over a long period. Waters decided to run in November 1971, and the final election was not until November of 1972. The primary was held in May, however, and in such a solidly Democratic district it was the primary that would determine the election. (The final election, in which Waters defeated his Republican opponent with 61 per cent of the vote, took place in November 1972. This discussion concerns only the primary and runoff races.)

The real kickoff for the campaign was a February meeting between the candidate, his campaign manager, and local party workers, party leaders from seven precincts, and candidates for leadership posts in five others, together with a state senate candidate whose campaign would be linked with Waters'. The outcome of that meeting was a series of decisions on campaign strategy, including plans for a precinct organization of the district.

The key decision made at that meeting — to have campaign workers contact every registered voter in the district before the primary — was to determine the nature of the campaign.

"Ann was convinced that block-walking was the only way to win," Waters states, and her view prevailed. With the exception of three conservative precincts which were written off, virtually every voter was reached by campaign volunteers. (There were 26,000 voters in the district.)

"We stressed that we wanted in-depth discussion with the people. We did not want people to just drop a leaflet," Ms. Lower said in discussing the campaign. "Our block-walkers were enthused. It's what kept the campaign going."

While Waters had originally pledged to walk every street of the district himself, he gave up on that idea after covering about 5 per cent of the district. Finding that his progress was too slow, and believing himself to be ineffective on a one to one basis, Waters decided that the best forum for him was a large group or rally. (He had been a champion debater.)

Having realized that the four black precincts would be crucial in determining the outcome of the primary, he did stick with the door to door tour in those areas.

Turning to what seemed his forte, Waters appeared before a series of large gatherings ranging in attendance from 150 to 2000. One of these was a rock concert at which he spoke alongside gubernatorial candidate Sissy Farenthold, whose candidacy rocked the Texas political establishment to its foundations.

For all the effort put into the Waters' campaign, there were numerous potential campaign tools it ignored. No headcount of Waters' supporters was attempted, nor did the campaign conduct a major effort to bring out the vote on election day. There was no effort to poll public opinion about the campaign.

In retrospect, Waters said he believed that a poll or a headcount would have been of great value. Having overestimated the response he was to get in the primary, he said he was shocked to be outpolled by the former legislator. The latter received 3518 to Waters' 3120, while the other four candidates received a combined total of 1600 votes. Fortunately for Waters, the crowded primary field meant that there would be a runoff in which he would have a second shot.

One aspect of the primary results that Waters might have discovered in advance was the fact that in the most liberal of the district's twenty-one precincts he received 300 fewer votes than Farenthold. The reason, he would learn, was that it was not generally realized there that he was more liberal than Farenthold. Similarly, Waters had been beaten in four precincts he thought were solidly for him and which he had taken for granted. While this failing was remedied before the runoff, it could have been avoided entirely by more careful study of voter attitudes. After his rude awakening in the primary, Waters ended up winning in the runoff with a vote of 5824 to 5030.

The significant point about Waters' campaign is that on a budget of $5000 he was able to run a six-month primary campaign that mobilized a broad coalition around a relatively radical platform, and that he won against an opponent estimated to have a budget of more than $20,000 at his disposal.

Equally important, that Waters' victory was not the fruit of a campaign put together at the spur of the moment: he had put enough time into earlier political activities so that he was familiar with his district and the issues affecting it. He also knew enough to seek the backing of other local leaders. While it was a matter of luck that he had the opportunity to run when he did, Waters had gone to great lengths to be ready for such an opportunity when it came.

Southfield, Michigan:
School Board Member Leonard Teicher

In contrast with Ron Waters' knowledge of the political landscape at the time of his decision to run, Leonard Teicher of Southfield, Michigan, was comparatively unaware of the local political situation when he began his first campaign in April of 1971. Though thoroughly acquainted with the issues affecting the schools, Teicher was at the time of his announcement unfamiliar with the influential coalition that would eventually put him in office.

"I looked upon the campaign as essentially a one-man effort with the help of a few friends," Teicher recalls. "I said I would spend $100 on the campaign, win or lose." In an electoral district containing close to 70,000 residents, Teicher's estimate of what would be required to win an election was modest indeed.

He did not know that in the seven weeks between his announcement and his election, he would become part of a two-man slate that would spend $2300, employ dozens of volunteers and be accused of introducing machine politics into a city where it was thought that school board races were "above politics."

This is not to say that Teicher was a political novice. A thirty-six-year-old attorney active in both professional associations and community affairs, he had long been involved in politics as a party worker. A volunteer in every presidential campaign since Adlai Stevenson's first effort, he was corresponding secretary of the Southfield Democratic Club at the time of his decision to seek a school board seat.

A native of nearby Detroit, he had lived in suburban Southfield only five years at the time of his election. In spite of his involvement in community affairs, it was not until three months before the election that he had thought seriously of running for office.

Three weeks before the filing deadline, only seven weeks before the election, Teicher mailed out a letter announcing his candidacy to the local papers, to PTA officials throughout the city, and to a number of influential citizens. He still thought of the campaign as a limited effort, and had not done any serious analysis of his chances of getting elected. "The odds were immaterial," he said.

Less than six weeks before the election he was contacted by the Southfield Educational Coalition and invited to appear at a meeting where candidates would seek the group's endorsement. Though this was the first time he had heard of the coalition, his attendance at that meeting would be the decisive event in his campaign. The coalition was an ad hoc group made up of the Southfield teachers' union, the Southfield Democratic Club, and two other groups of citizens concerned about education.

Teicher won the coalition's endorsement as candidate for the one year remaining in a term unfinished by a board member who had resigned before completing the usual four years. A second candidate, Paul Blinkilde, won the endorsement for a full term. Since Blinkilde's endorsement for the full term had been a virtual certainty (he had been the coalition's candidate in a previous race), Teicher's decision to seek the one year term instead of the four year term was crucial. Had he sought the longer term, he most likely would not have been endorsed. "The endorsement was vital. I would not have won without the endorsement," he said later.

The endorsement was only the beginning of the coalition's support. Teicher was subsequently asked if he would run with Blinkilde on a slate receiving the coalition's full backing. The person who asked him to do so was a public relations man at a firm which specialized in political campaigns.

"It suddenly dawned on me that he's got fantastic credentials, and he's offering his services," Teicher said about the offer. "It also dawned on me that they were talking about spending $1000 or $1500." Of course, he accepted. "This changed my concept of the campaign radically."

With his spot on the slate, Teicher also received the services of a campaign manager, a public relations adviser, a network of campaigners who had worked in past elections, and a treasury. (Roughly half of the $2300 spent by the slate was raised through personal solicitation, but the teachers' union contributed $800 and the candidates $100 each.)

Opposing Teicher and Blinkilde were a slate backed by an ad hoc conservative alliance and three individual candidates unaffiliated with any important organizations. Roughly four weeks remained in the campaign after the Teicher-Blinkilde

slate was formed. Before the coalition's campaign got underway, a campaign against the coalition slate had been launched
from an unexpected source.

Deploring the fact that the coalition had endorsed Teicher
and Blinkilde "so early before the election," a local newspaper
editorialized that the endorsement was a "publicity gimmick"
unworthy of Southfield politics. It also played up the fact that
the coalition had the services of a public relations man. The
implication was that the mere existence of an organized political entity was inappropriate in a school board race in Southfield. Teicher, Blinkilde, and the coalition were regarded as
having violated a local taboo against political sophistication.
Even the fact that Teicher had announced his candidacy before the filing deadline was held against him. While the issue
died down in time for Teicher and Blinkilde to win the election (not without further discussion of how much money they
were spending, which was about the same as what the other
slate spent), the incident serves as a good example of how sensitive a candidate must be to the traditions and biases of his
district.

Though their turned out to be the first Southfield school
board race in which any real campaigning occurred, the
Teicher-Blinkilde campaign was fairly simple in any other
terms. The campaign's only expenditures were for postage, literature, and lawn signs. Voter registration and canvassing
were not done at all, and the candidates' major activities were
attending affairs such as coffee hours and candidates' nights.
Volunteers were used for mailing and distributing literature,
and in a get-out-the-vote effort.

Bringing voters to the polls was the main challenge. "We
knew where the liberal precincts were," he said, "and we went
on the assumption that in any liberal precinct, three out of
four voters would be favorable." Since the city is divided
neatly into one section occupied by liberal newcomers and an-

other occupied by conservative oldtimers, "we really considered the election to be won or lost in half the city, and we concentrated on that half."

Teicher and Blinkilde were distinguished from their opponents less by particular issues than by the fact that they were presented as liberals and their opponents as conservatives. A focal point in the election was whether the existing 4-3 liberal majority on the board would survive. When Teicher and Blinkilde won by comfortable margins the liberal edge was increased to 5-2.

Chapel Hill, North Carolina: Mayor Howard Lee

When Howard Lee became Mayor of Chapel Hill in May, 1969, his election constituted a revolution in the town's politics. Howard Lee's victory made him the only black mayor of a predominantly white town in the South. (Chapel Hill is only 10 per cent black.)

Lee's election also was the first occasion in which the University of North Carolina's domination of town politics had been challenged.

Finally, as Lee put it, "This was the first time that Chapel Hill had a real election campaign."

The last point helps explain the first two: Lee and his supporters ran a campaign that was as intensive and thorough as it was controversial. As an example of how aggressively he campaigned, Lee and his wife attended some 363 coffee hours in three months, or an average of four a day, with ten to twenty guests at each. This in a town of 27,000!

Lee was an articulate and knowledgeable candidate who could expect to win an election, but his victory was by no means assured. In addition to being black (race was inevitably an issue), he had made himself known as "Howard Lee the blockbuster" when in 1966 he had waged a successful six-month battle to become the first black to buy a home in a white Chapel Hill neighborhood. Lee was new to Chapel Hill, having lived there only five years at the time of his election. His opponent was a long-time resident who had been an alderman for nine years and who was well known as a newspaper columnist and an official of the University's alumni association.

Less than six months before the election, Lee had not given a thought to running for office. The first time he considered running was in November 1968, when a friend suggested that he seek a spot on the board of aldermen. That proposal was the outcome of a meeting of black leaders who were trying to decide how to counter the board's refusal to pass an open-housing ordinance.

Lee was still thinking about that proposal when at another meeting of black and white liberals it was suggested that in addition to running a black for alderman a white liberal should be recruited to run for mayor.

That suggestion rankled Lee, who had grown annoyed with comments that it was "too soon" for Chapel Hill to have a black mayor. "If we are going to shake the system, we should shake it good," Lee argued, suggesting that a black seek the mayor's seat. Lee's view prevailed and a tentative agreement to seek a black candidate was made. By December, a third meeting occurred, at which it was suggested that Lee should be the candidate. He agreed to think it over.

Before Lee was able to make his decision, it was more or less made for him when a friend leaked the plan to a newspaper editor and the next issue of the paper had a story headlined "Black to Run for Mayor." Still unsure he wanted to run, Lee had not even discussed the idea with his wife. Within three weeks he had discussed the possibility with fifty to sixty people, including other politicians and fund-raising sources.

Hoping to recruit a nine-member campaign committee, Lee

invited a group of twenty-two to a meeting at his house in late
January. He still had no organization and the election was
only three months away. Fifty-four people showed up for that
meeting, including another candidate. The group gave him its
unanimous support and the campaign was under way. In the
next week $1000 was raised and by the end of the second week
200 workers had been recruited.

From that point on the Lee campaign was a model of grassroots organizing. In addition to the candidate's own formidable round of coffee hours, volunteers went door to door to contact every registered voter in Chapel Hill. Several hundred
new voters were registered, and a list of sympathetic voters was
compiled for use on election day. Position papers, campaign
newsletters, and other material were mimeographed and delivered to both general and selected lists of voters. Most of the
$5000 spent by the organization was raised in donations of $20
or less.

"The really marvelous thing about that campaign was the
fact that all kinds of people of all ages participated," said Ann
Barnes, a local Democratic Party worker who managed the
campaign. (Her husband, a writer and photographer, did the
campaign's public relations on a volunteer basis.) "It just
caught on and people were eager to be part of it."

"The greatest single asset of the campaign was Howard
himself," she also said. "He was a great campaigner and a
great candidate."

A voter registration campaign and the wide interest the
election attracted resulted in a record turnout on the May 6
election. Lee won by a vote of 2566 to 2116. A third factor
contributing to the high turnout was the massive election day
drive the organization staged.

Lee's opponent had not been a pushover, though as Lee
said, "He took me lightly," and did not begin campaigning
until well after Lee had. The opposition had the backing of

local businessmen, of the town's newspaper, and of a large block of Chapel Hill residents who had given him the aldermen's seat year after year. Lee estimates that his opponent had as much as four times as much money at his disposal, noting that he doubled Lee's efforts in radio and newspaper advertising.

The Lee organization was the chief factor in his victory, but the campaign was not based on organization alone. The candidates were clearly distinguished by their stands on issues, and race was one of the more critical issues. Ironically, Lee was at first criticized for not being really black: opponents played up the fact that he lived in a white neighborhood and attended a white church. "Unfortunately the blacks ate it up," Lee said. That charge was dispensed with when Lee addressed a black church group on the subject. Similarly, a rumor that Lee had a white mistress was banished by a white woman working for Lee who jokingly dismissed it in an interview on a radio talk show. Finally, the Chapel Hill *Weekly* editorialized that Lee could only win if he did so by getting a sympathy vote from guilt-ridden whites.

In concluding that inverted racism was the determining factor in the campaign, however, the paper ignored both the efforts of Lee's supporters and the nature of the issues in Lee's platform. It also overlooked his considerable experience: Lee was a board member on a Chapel Hill anti-poverty program, a member of the legislative committee of the local Democratic Party, and president of the Eastern North Carolina chapter of the National Association of Social Workers.

Lee was advocating major changes in the running of Chapel Hill, changes which his opponent was generally against. Lee advocated:

1. Changing the role of the mayor from the ceremonial one it had always been to one of strong and active leadership.

2. Establishing a municipal public transportation system.

3. Building housing for low-income people.

4. Establishing a municipal redevelopment program to benefit the town's black neighborhoods.

5. Ending the University of North Carolina's ownership of the town's electricity, water, and telephone systems.

6. Passing an open housing ordinance.

Lee pushed for these and other major innovations in Chapel Hill government, while his opponent remained on the defensive, advocating a continuation of the status quo.

Only a few months after the thought of running for office first occurred to him, Lee became mayor of Chapel Hill with a mandate to carry out his progressive program. His entry into office, however, was in many respects not his own doing. Had he not been active in community affairs, he would almost certainly not have been asked to run. Had he not been able to draw on such a wide group of supporters, he could not have won.

Wayne, New Jersey:
City Councilman David Waks

As with Lee and Teicher, the election of David Waks as a city councilman in Wayne, N. J., was not the long-awaited climax of a calculated series of efforts to gather experience and contacts. It was the result of a relatively spontaneous decision that took place after it became apparent that he might have something to offer as a candidate.

Three years prior to his decision to run, Waks had not been involved in political or civic organizations. Once involved, he took one small step after another up the ladder that finally put him in office. In this respect, Waks' route to office is perhaps typical of that followed by most local politicians.

Early in 1968, David Waks was two years out of law school, having lived in Wayne only since beginning his practice in nearby Paterson. Less than four years later he would be a member of the Wayne city council, a fact somewhat directly attributable to his decision to campaign for Eugene McCarthy in the New Jersey primary of 1968. (Howard Lee had also entered electoral politics by becoming a McCarthy volunteer.)

It was the McCarthy campaign that introduced Waks to Wayne's political activists. A year after learning the art of canvassing in that campaign, Waks helped manage the campaign of a friend who was seeking the mayor's seat. Also in 1969, he became well enough known to win a seat on the Passaic County Democratic Committee. Between 1968 and 1971 he became a key figure in the group of liberal insurgents who reformed the Wayne Democratic Club and began pressing for reform of city government.

Along with his work in the local party, the second factor which set the stage for Waks' candidacy was his participation in the formation of a tenants' rights organization. A resident of a garden apartment complex, Waks helped form one of six tenants' associations that later banded together as the Wayne Tenants' Council. By the time of his decision to run for office, he had created a useful base of power among his neighbors and party workers.

Simultaneous with his political education, Waks had become increasingly concerned about the future of Wayne, a city approximately of 52,000 which retained some of its former rural character despite being less than twenty miles from Newark. With developers riding roughshod over the city's remaining green areas, Wayne seemed in danger of becoming just one more patch of crowded housing developments, highways, and shopping centers. Due to the lax attitude of city officials toward the rapid spread of construction projects, what remained of Wayne's woodlands and farms was quickly disappearing. "I wanted Wayne to slow down and take a look at where it was going," Waks recalled.

As the time for the 1971 city council election approached,

all of these factors converged and led to his decision to run. "I was popular in the party. I felt that I had the support of the people who were in the fifth ward in the Democratic club. I felt that my identification with the tenants' cause would be of help." By April, he had decided to run, though without seeking prior support or discussing his candidacy with anyone, other than with a close friend who was also a tenant leader. The Democratic primary would be in June and the final in November.

Since he was seeking one of the six city council seats elected by ward, he would have to direct his campaign to only 12,000 of Wayne's 52,000 residents, a distinct advantage for a new candidate. Of the voters in Waks' ward, about 60 per cent lived in single family homes, but the rest lived in 1667 apartment units: every apartment building in Wayne was in his ward, another important advantage.

In spite of his three years' experience in local party affairs, Waks took a somewhat amateurish approach to his campaign in the beginning. While one of his primary opponents had workers gathering signatures on nomination petitions for two months, Waks began late and made his announcement by simply writing a letter to the screening committee of the Wayne Municipal Democratic Committee, asking for its support. "If I had it to do over again, I would have had petitions out," he later said. "I didn't even know how much money I was going to spend. We didn't sit down beforehand and figure out how many mailings we were going to have. It was a lack of experience in running."

Virtually all of the $459 he spent on the primary and the $1450 he spent on the general election came out of his own pocket. "I felt at the time that a campaign could be run for a minimum amount. I did not make an active effort to find funds. I didn't want anyone to feel obliged to give a monetary contribution. If someone will give you his time it's worth a lot more," Waks said.

Because of his reluctance to make demands on others, Waks did not organize as extensive a campaign as he might have during the primary race. A party worker volunteered to be his campaign manager and organized a group of workers who prepared and delivered leaflets. Three pieces of literature went out to each voter before the June primary. For the most part it was a very personal campaign, in which Waks began knocking on doors and by election day had visited virtually every registered Democrat and independent in the ward. Except for the three sets of leaflets, the door to door tour was his major effort in the primary race. "I felt I was doing enough to win without asking people to do more than I had to," he said. After trying his hand at a few coffee hours, he gave up on those because of the small turnouts: "It was a waste of time because I could have been out knocking on forty doors."

As low-keyed as Waks' campaign was, it was not taking place in a vacuum. In addition to being known as "the tenant's candidate" (a label both he and the tenants resented, but which nevertheless made him known among apartment dwellers), Waks was also the choice of the newly reformed Wayne Democratic Organization. After he received the endorsement of the reform Democrats, his chief opponent got the support of another organization recently created by Democratic regulars. The city councilman race thus became a battle between liberals and the long-reigning local machine. The contrast in the two candidates' styles was clear on the night before the primary, when Waks went out knocking on doors while his opponent drove a motorcade through the ward, waving from his car to nonexistent crowds. The next day, Waks won with a vote of 422 to 302; a third candidate took 58 votes. Though the 782 voters who cast Democratic ballots represented less than 20 per cent of the ward's registered voters, it was nevertheless a record turnout for a municipal primary. "I would attribute that in large part to an awakening of the tenants rather than to my own popularity," Waks said.

Turning to the general election, Waks determined to take full advantage of the tenants' support: "Shortly after the primary I had decided that one of the keys would be registration of the people in garden apartments." Information on registration was printed up and members of the Tenants' Council began locating unregistered voters while also gathering support for Waks. In all, some 500 apartment dwellers were registered to vote between June and the September 23 deadline. Considering the fact that his final victory was by a margin of 526 votes, Waks' decision to concentrate on registration was unmistakably wise.

As in the primary, he again relied heavily on personal door to door campaigning. In the last six weeks before the final election he visited approximately 1700 of the ward's 3200 residences, skipping only the homes of unregistered voters and the residents of his Republican opponent's home precinct. (There was also an independent candidate in the final, the same machine Democrat defeated in the primary.)

By September, Waks' corps of volunteers had grown to about eighty members, their efforts being dedicated primarily to voter registration and delivering campaign literature. In making his house to house visits, Waks had personally compiled a list of 1000 voters he considered committed to him and this list was readied for the use of canvassers on election day.

On election day, campaign workers at each of the ward's three polling places kept track of which Waks' voters had appeared, so that those who had not voted could be contacted. More than forty workers took part in the election day effort. Temporary headquarters had been set up in each apartment complex and a telephone pool had been organized to reach voters in less densely populated areas. Waks' victory was clearcut: compared to his 1424 votes, the Republican candidate received 898 and the independent Democrat 480.

Of the six candidates discussed in this chapter, David Waks

made the least use of a formal organization and had the least direct support from groups outside his campaign. In spite of his self-reliant approach to running a campaign, it is clear that his election was made possible by his previous "toil in the vineyards." Two of the major issues in the campaign, tenants' rights and clean government, were directly related to his work in other organizations prior to the campaign. The volunteer support he received grew out of his work in those organizations. Waks' candidacy underscores the fact that it is a rare candidate who makes a successful try at running for office without having established a political base before running.

Madison, Wisconsin: Assemblywoman Marjorie "Midge" Miller

Midge Miller was a definite underdog when she decided in the spring of 1970 to seek the Wisconsin Assembly seat of a conservative Republican ten-year veteran. Only once before had a Democrat represented the West Side Madison district, whose 60,000 residents were mainly upper-middle-class professionals. Besides being a Democrat and a woman, Ms. Miller was well known as a peace activist and had been a prominent figure in the McCarthy campaign.

"Some people felt that since I was considered to be liberal this would make it more difficult for me than for a conservative Democrat," she said. "My theory was that that just wasn't so. Why would people cross over from their own party to get a candidate just like the one they had? The only way they would cross over would be if there was some strong appeal of the candidate in the other party."

Her decision to run was based more on faith in herself and the electorate than on the district's known political preferences: "I think if I had ever looked at the statistics and realized how unlikely it was that any Democrat would win, I probably wouldn't have run."

Underdog or not, Ms. Miller was no novice. In addition to having held several party posts, she had campaigned for Democrats on every level since 1957. She had run the state campaign office for McCarthy in 1968, had gone to Chicago as a delegate, and was national vice-chairman of the New Democratic Coalition. In her private career, she had been an assistant dean at the University of Wisconsin for six years. She was also the mother of nine children.

In spite of the heavily Republican character of her district, she was in a good position to build an effective organization. "I felt that my long years of active social concern had developed a lot of friends and a lot of people who had some respect for me." She also thought her gender might be more of an asset than a liability: "Contrary to some of my opponents who felt that my being a woman was a disadvantage, I had thought that even in 1970 there would be some women who would cross over to vote for another woman."

Entering the race in May, Ms. Miller was the third Democrat to announce. A fourth made his announcement shortly thereafter, guaranteeing that the September primary would require an intensive campaign. The other Democrats were sure to have solid support: one was a Madison city councilman, another a former Democratic Party county chairman, and the third was a county board supervisor. This was Ms. Miller's first try for public office.

Midge Miller waged an extremely personal campaign. She gathered a large volunteer staff, eventually drawing hundreds of Madison residents into the campaign. "My main contacts were on a person to person basis, either speaking before groups or speaking at coffee hours, answering questions. Where I spoke, people were very supportive, and I encouraged them to participate and help. We had literally hundreds of volunteers as a result of these coffees and meetings."

"Going to coffees is a risky way to campaign," she notes, "because you're strictly on your own, without benefit of any of the 'packaging' devices used so extensively in conventional campaigning. But that's what's so good about it from a voter's point of view. What better way is there to find out about a candidate than to question him or her in your neighbor's living room?" By the end of the campaign, she had attended more than 150 coffees and other small meetings.

Despite the fact that she had no paid staff and bought no advertising on radio or television, the Miller campaign ended up costing almost $10,000. Most of that was spent on an array of high-quality literature, including five pieces hand-carried to 20,000 homes each, and other pieces sent to smaller special interest groups. The renting of an office facilitated work with volunteers.

"It became very much the 'in' thing to go to a Miller coffee and people were very generous. It is a middle- and upper-class area and therefore if people are convinced of the merits of a candidate they have the resources to give. Much of the money was obtained by mailings requesting help. We had three major money-raising events and several small ones. We did an interesting thing: we got away from the chicken dinner kind of thing and had a country fair and a Halloween party. Particularly in these two cases, people were encouraged to bring their children. We raised close to a thousand dollars at each."

In addition to being a grassroots effort, the Miller campaign was intensely issue-oriented. In her literature and in her activities, Ms. Miller made the campaign an educational as well as a political effort. Prior to the primary she scheduled fourteen public meetings devoted to a single subject each, with subjects ranging from Indian affairs to transportation. At each meeting she shared the floor with experts to discuss the various subjects.

She won the primary by a convincing margin, taking 3472

of the 8450 Democratic votes cast, 1200 more than her nearest competitor. Ms. Miller attributes part of her success to the fact that she stood out so clearly from the rest of the candidates: "At the meetings where all the candidates spoke I had a very real advantage because I was the only woman. The men were, except for the Republican, close to the same age and size, and rarely did basic differences come out in the kinds of questions that were related to this particular campaign. Being a woman, being new, being a bit more iconoclastic, I was somewhat more interesting to the voter and to the press."

The final election offered the voters an equally clear choice. In their records, their outlooks and their personalities, Ms. Miller and her Republican opponent were worlds apart. Ms. Miller's appeal was helped by the fact that the Republican-oriented paper which formerly supported the opposition candidate did not support either candidate.

The election results indicated that the Republican habit was still strong and that every bit of effort the Miller campaign put out had been needed. She ended up winning with 11,597 votes, only 1300 more than her opponent.

An interesting sequel to Midge Miller's campaign is the fact that in her try for re-election to a second term in 1972 she received the endorsement of the Republican, the Democratic, and the student newspapers. She received 72 per cent of the total vote and defeated the Republican challenger in every precinct in the district.

Chicago, Illinois:
Alderman Dick Simpson

Dick Simpson's campaign for a seat on the Chicago city council is the most sophisticated and most expensive campaign under discussion here. This is so even though his ward, with roughly 66,000 residents, was smaller than the districts of two other candidates we have discussed. Because it was waged against the Daley machine, the Simpson campaign *had* to be large and sophisticated. Techniques used in this campaign were nevertheless no different from those used by other candidates mentioned here.

A political science professor at the University of Illinois, Simpson entered electoral politics as a McCarthy volunteer in Chicago in 1968. By the end of that campaign he had become state campaign manager and was permanently committed to political organizing. Shortly afterwards he helped form the Independent Precinct Organization (IPO), a citywide independent coalition which attempted to build a strong enough counter-machine to combat Daley. As executive director of IPO, Simpson worked in a series of campaigns in roles ranging from precinct worker to campaign manager.

By the fall of 1970, Simpson was eager to try the role of candidate himself, and anxious not to resign himself to working always in the campaigns of others. "I didn't want to get boxed in, and I wanted to test whether it was possible for me to win public office." He was also beginning to be frustrated with working for candidates who did not entirely represent his own way of thinking: "I deal with issues differently from other independents in the council. I tend to take a stronger position and polarize a situation more than it was previously," he later stated.

Just as Simpson warmed up to the idea of running, the boundaries of the ward in which he was living, near Lincoln Park, were realigned in a manner that put him in the ward of another independent alderman he had helped to elect. Not long after he had scrapped the idea of running, Simpson relates, "I was contacted by a citizens' search committee from the Lakeview community, which was north of where I lived but in the same general area of the city, and I was asked to run there."

The latter ward, he found, "had been specifically gerryman-
dered by the Democratic party to be impossible for an independent candidate to win." In an attempt to fragment the impact of the liberal neighborhoods along Lake Michigan, the
portion of the Jewish community in the redistricted ward had
been reduced, while the size of other machine-dominated
areas, mainly Puerto Rican and German, had been increased.

Even with the gerrymander, Simpson believed, "The district
was small enough so that an all-out campaign against the
strongest machine in the nation could be waged and still have
a chance of winning." Despite the additional handicaps of
having to move into the district at the last minute and beginning the campaign late, Simpson decided to run. The committee which asked him to run had assured him of sufficient
financial and material support. Independent campaigns had
been run in the district before, indicating that experienced
workers were available. "I knew that I could get good precinct coordinators, that I could get a staff together. I was convinced that with the kind of manpower available, it was a
good enough test of whether I could win, and that it was a test
that the independent movement had to undertake with a
major candidate." Having made his decision, Simpson took
an apartment in his new ward on November 20 and began the
campaign the next day. The election would be held just three
months later, on February 23.

On November 21, the search committee that had recruited
Simpson produced a group of fifty persons at a meeting which
constituted the campaign kickoff. By election day several hundred workers would grow around this base and the campaign
would have a group of volunteers in every precinct. It would
also raise more than $20,000, spend $25,000 and win the campaign with a budget deficit of $3500. (Simpson said this was
the least expensive winning campaign ever run by an independent alderman.)

After the first organizational meeting, workers were sent out to gather signatures on nominating petitions needed to put Simpson's name on the ballot. Instead of obtaining the relative handful needed, they wound up with 3500. Campaign literature was then sent out to the people who had signed the petitions, in order to raise funds and recruit additional workers.

When the petition drive was finished, a voter registration drive was started, eventually putting approximately one thousand Simpson voters on the rolls. (He ended up winning by a vote of 8828 to 7336.) Canvassers later came up with a list of approximately 7000 Simpson backers who were called to the polls on election day.

While volunteers went about the street work, Simpson made the rounds of the meetings of some fifty community organizations whose leaders or members he wooed. He also sought the endorsements of independent politicians and political groups opposed to the Daley machine. By the end of the campaign he had the endorsements of groups as varied as the National Organization of Women, the Republican Party, and the Independent Democratic Coalition.

"I had a whole spectrum of endorsements which indicated to the voter that this was going to be one of the major campaigns, that it had the kind of support that meant it was going to be a real battle, that I wasn't just standing up and going to run. It's important that some kind of credibility be established, and about the only way to do it is by endorsements," Simpson later said.

If Simpson's stature as a candidate was established in part by means of endorsements, it was also enhanced by the attention he attracted in other ways. Taking advantage of every citizen's right to file proposals with the city council, he entered a measure that would have taken away Mayor Daley's power to appoint school board members. While the proposal was obviously doomed, it won news coverage and established the fact that Simpson was indeed independent. "I could say that I was going to be an independent voice in the city council and not a rubber stamp. My opponent was caught because every other alderman who had ever been elected by the Democratic Party had voted as he was told to."

Simpson earned support by taking on a major towing firm whose employees were known throughout the ward for their habit of breaking into or damaging the cars they towed, and for occasionally beating up irate car owners. Simpson took citizen complaints to the state attorney's office and filed suit against the firm. That controversy got frequent headlines in the last days of the campaign, winning votes from residents suddenly grateful for real representation. In this case as on other issues, Simpson told the voters, "Look, I will do something about these sorts of things and my opponent is doing nothing." His election indicated that the message got across.

12

On Being a Candidate

To LIST THE CHORES that occupy a candidate's time in his weeks or months of campaigning is a relatively simple matter. But to conclude that being a candidate involves nothing more than delivering speeches, shaking hands, or ironing out the details of a position paper is to ignore deeper and broader aspects of being a politician. There is much more to being a candidate than what is outwardly visible, much that happens within him and much that happens *to* him.

Though we have already spoken of the candidate's role as if it were a simple and straightforward assembly of tasks, a candidate plays several different roles. Each of these demands slightly different talents, and some of these roles are conflicting.

Politicians are frequently accused of attempting to be "all things to all people," and in a sense a political candidate must be many things. Anyone who attempts to win the loyalty of widely different political factions must develop an ability to alter his style or approach to relate to the audience of the moment. The tragedy of politics is that this necessity sometimes leads a political figure to alter his ideas and his principles as well as his style.

By gathering together his campaign organization, a candidate becomes first of all the leader of a minority faction which seeks to bring a larger community around to its views.

Though a candidate should leave the work of managing his organization to others, his role in the organization is still the primary leadership role.

A candidate must set the tone of his organization and give it a reason for being. He must somehow arouse the confidence and trust of those who are working for him and he must inspire the enthusiasm that marks a really motivated campaign.

Beyond demonstrating to his supporters that he represents their sentiments and deserves their trust, a candidate must convey what can only be described as a "winner's psychology." Only if a candidate himself believes that he can and will win is it possible to develop the spirit essential to a winning campaign. A candidate who does not generate a sense of conviction and determination, who does not give off some kind of spark, cannot expect motivation to arise spontaneously from elsewhere in his organization.

This is not to say that every candidate must have the charisma of a Kennedy. It means that the esprit necessary to a successful campaign does not just happen: it starts with a candidate willing to work and dedicated to winning. It then spreads outward through those closest to him, until the impact is finally felt by those outside the campaign. A candidate's will to win — or his lack of it — is mirrored in a hundred details of his own behavior and of the standards of performance which he applies to his workers. A candidate who fails to keep appointments, who allows his headquarters to turn into a shambles, or who flies off the handle in dealing with campaign workers, is not going to attract support and create a winning team. In turn, he is not going to win the confidence of the public.

Discipline is an important factor in the make-up of a winning candidate, since a campaign will be disciplined only if the candidate himself is disciplined and demands a high standard of performance from himself and from his staff. Any organization is only as good as its leadership. The candidate's leadership role, even if it is mainly leadership by example, is one to which he must pay great attention.

The difficulty of a candidate's leadership role is compounded by the pressures put on him by his other roles as public figure and community leader: the one role laying his whole life open to public inspection and discussion, the other requiring that he give up much of himself as part of the job of serving the public.

The business of being a public figure requires that a candidate tolerate pressures and attacks that no private citizen would willingly accept. A candidate can expect to have his morality questioned, his personal foibles held up to ridicule, and his past indiscretions publicly aired. It is also fairly frequent that even a candidate's wife or children will be publicly maligned.

A candidate must also sacrifice much in order to fill his role as a community leader, in terms of both his personality and his time and energy. Being a candidate takes a lot out of an individual's private life by demanding that he meet public duties at times when he would rather be with his family and friends. What is perhaps more important is that being a candidate sometimes requires an individual to put aside some of his most cherished ideas and change many of his priorities in response to public demand.

Just by becoming a candidate, an individual announces that he is willing to compromise some of his best ideas in deference to the public will. A candidate must be receptive to the beliefs and preferences of his constituents, even if he does not finally accept them, and must be willing to seek out positions on public issues which answer the concerns of his constituency. He must also be willing to focus on issues that are important to his constituency at times when his heart is really elsewhere. Neither of these statements means that a candidate must "sell out." What is meant is that a candidate's own concerns and beliefs are not all that matters: an individual who purports to represent thousands of voters must be *willing* to represent them. There may be some issues that a candidate sees as moral issues on which he cannot bend. But most political issues are not moral issues and usually a candidate must be willing to meet his constituency halfway.

Each of a candidate's roles is thus liable to pull him in somewhat different directions: as the leader of his campaign he must crystallize the wishes of his supporters, while as community leader he must be willing to speak for a wider constituency: as public figure he must subject himself to pressures that he would otherwise not accept. In being a candidate, any individual puts himself at the center of an emotional and intellectual whirlpool. This fact assumes greater importance when one considers how enormous the demands on a candidate's resources can be in even a small campaign.

Running for a hotly contested office with a district of as few as 20,000 or 30,000 voters can easily involve months of full-time campaigning, preceded by further months of precampaign activity. During the campaign, the candidate may spend the greater part of his waking hours on the march from one political affair to another: knocking on doors, addressing neighborhood coffee hours, working with campaign staff. Rather than tapering off, the workload and the pressure increase steadily as election day nears.

These activities are not merely physically and intellectually demanding. They are a great emotional strain, since a candidate must constantly shift psychological gears as he moves from one activity to another. He must adjust his style, mood, and tempo to correspond to the situation at hand: shaking hands on a street corner, discussing his ideas with a major contributor, speaking to a crowd at a rally or a dinner. He must perform well in each of these activities, often in rapid succession, all the while fighting off the emotional impact of occasional setbacks and meeting responsibilities toward a family or friends. Projected over a period of several weeks or months, this routine can constitute a grueling test of his dedication and stamina.

It is easy to understand why the role of the candidate is taken on by so few citizens. Getting elected is an arduous process, a burden heavier than most citizens are willing to bear. Campaigning is as morally and psychologically demanding as it is expensive. It is also as likely to consume a candidate's ideals and energy without yielding any return as it is to reward him.

An American political campaign typically amounts to a trial by ordeal in which the candidate who emerges as the winner is not the one who has the "right" viewpoint on issues, but the one who combines a variety of skills and a temperament equal to the strains of campaigning with whatever ideas he has on the issues.

These considerations help explain one of the fundamental errors of liberal and radical thinking about American politics: the tendency to think that if the public will just listen to the ideas of a candidate with a good program, he will get elected. A candidate is not just a lecturer or an essayist: he must be an administrator, an actor, and a quick judge of people and situations. He must also have a high tolerance for frustration and plenty of energy. Campaigning involves far more than letting the people hear what the candidate thinks.

If elections were based solely on issues, it would be sufficient to have every candidate publish his position papers or appear on television for an hour or two. The voters could then be sent to the polls and the process quickly ended, without the months of grueling work that make up a campaign. The entire election process could be compressed into a week or two.

The campaign is designed to reveal much more about a

candidate than what he thinks. In putting him under severe and constant pressure, a campaign reveals more than a candidate's opinion. It also tests his skills as an organizer, an executive, and a public relations expert.

The need for a candidate to display such a diversity of skills and qualities explains the blandness of the usual political personality. Rather than wonder at the small number of bright and dedicated leaders we get, we should wonder how we get so many. The campaign process undoubtedly scares off a lot of modest or sensitive potential leaders who might perform superbly in office but who are unable to submit themselves to the ordeal of campaigning.

Despite this weakness, the campaign process has two virtues that more than compensate for its deficiencies. First is the fact that the tens of thousands of political campaigns that occur in the United States each year permit untold numbers of citizens to play a vital role in determining what our political leadership will be. With more than half a million elected officials running for office periodically, there are constant opportunities for every citizen to shape the political process and alter the course of the nation.

It may be that the wrong people are involved in these half a million campaigns, that those who would make our best leaders stay away from the political process. American liberals and radicals, for all their idealism, have often been content to denounce "the system" and leave the field of government to conservatives or, worse, to incompetents. If our political system is dominated by any one group of citizens, it is those who happen to have worked hardest to gain control of it.

The campaign system also performs the invaluable function of forcing our leaders to learn from the electorate as well as to teach or to guide it. More than anything else, a candidate's political campaign is an opportunity for him to grow — to become more sensitive to the problems and prejudices of his constituents, to go beyond his own theories to an understanding of the very real people they would affect, and to take these lessons of the campaign into office with him. An American political candidate is forced to go directly to the people, to answer to them, and to seek their endorsement. As a result, he is far more likely to respond to their needs in performing the duties of his office than if he were able to acquire office without confronting the people whose will he is supposed to reflect.

This advantage of the campaign system has begun to be lost as our society becomes more complex. The size of our communities and the sophistication of our technology have grown to the point where it has become rare for a candidate to campaign in person. The decrease in contact between candidate and voter has led to a widening gap between the needs of the people and the ideas and priorities of their political leaders. Media campaigning has separated the public from its candidates and thus from its government.

The political campaign based on citizen involvement is a reaction against this trend, an attempt to break down the barriers of distance and technology. It combines economic advantage for the candidate with the desirable effect of bringing the candidate and the electorate closer together. In doing this, it serves both the public and the candidate, by intensifying the growth process he undergoes in his campaign, by identifying him more closely with his community, and by bringing him to the point where he has earned the leadership role he will assume in office.

There is no doubt that the print and electronic media are a permanent part of political life in America. To one degree or another, every candidate may be forced by the sheer size of his electoral district to use the mass media. The question is to what extent the reliance on mass media is due to a desire to avoid facing the public. The degree to which a candidate tries to meet the public directly and to prove his worth is a clear measure of his faith in the public and his desire to truly represent the public. The degree to which he relies on expensive media techniques to manipulate the public is an indication of his cynicism, distrust, and even contempt for the public.

In the final analysis, a politician's commitment to democracy is measured by his courage and candor in confronting the public with his true convictions on controversial matters. Anyone who believes in democracy must be willing to deal openly with the public on sensitive issues, though the public may be wary, hostile, and even unwilling to deal honestly with those issues itself. And a vital part of such openness is a willingness to face the public in person, however difficult and demanding that may be.

The moral and psychological aspects of being a candidate have been the subject of countless books by politicians and political observers from Niccolò Machiavelli to Richard Nixon, and there is no need for us to pursue those topics further here.

The purpose of this closing chapter has been to emphasize again that political behavior is always integrally related to political philosophy. A candidate's campaign style and his approach to the public are unmistakable indicators of his true political outlook.

The campaign techniques discussed here are recommended not merely because they work — other approaches also work — but because they are techniques that embody the democratic spirit in which this nation was founded. Neither the "new politics" techniques we favor nor the commitment to truly democratic action they reflect is unique in the nation's history. What is new in the "new politics" is the reawakening of citizen participation in politics on every level. In providing a manual for "new politicians," we hope to make this reawakening to some small extent more easy to achieve.

Index

39144

JK
2283
A9

Atkins, Chester G.

Getting elected

DATE			

© THE BAKER & TAYLOR CO.